Cabins, Canoes and Campfires

Guidelines for Establishing a Summer Camp for Children with Autism Spectrum Disorders

Cabins, Canoes and Campfires

Guidelines for Establishing a Summer Camp for Children with Autism Spectrum Disorders

Jill Hudson

Foreword by Brenda Smith Myles

Autism Asperger Publishing Co.
P.O. Box 23173
Shawnee Mission, Kansas 66283-0173
www.asperger.net

P.O. Box 23173
Shawnee Mission, Kansas 66283-0173
www.asperger.net

Publisher's Cataloging-in-Publication
(Provided by Quality Books, Inc.)

Hudson, Jill.
Cabins, canoes and campfire : guidelines for establishing a summer camp for children with autism spectrum disorders / Jill Hudson ; foreword by Brenda Smith Myles.
p. cm.
Includes bibliographical references.
ISBN 1-931282-77-3
LCCN: 2005926998

1. Camps for children with mental disabilities.
2. Autism in children. 3. Asperger's syndrome.
I. Myles, Brenda Smith. II. Title.

GV197.H3H83 2005 618.92'898206
QBI05-600052

This book is designed in Wendy and Frutiger.

Printed in the United States of America.

*This book is dedicated
to all children who continue
to thrive summer after summer
at camp.*

Table of Contents

Preface ix

Foreword xi

Introduction 1
- Value of Camp for Children with Autism Spectrum Disorders 1
  - Social Skills 2
  - Communication Skills 2
  - Repetitive/Idiosyncratic Behaviors and Special Interests 2
  - Sensory System 3
  - Motor Skills 3
  - Perception and Relating to the Environment 3
- Purpose of This Book 4

Chapter 1: Creating a Camp Plan 7
- Determining the Concept 7
- Sharing the Vision 8
- Leadership Team 8
  - Timeline 8
- Choosing a Facility 10
  - Location and Physical Layout 10
  - Program – Activities 12
  - Campground Staff 12
  - Mixed-Gender Cabins 13
- Developing a Policy 13
  - Insurance 14
- Developing the Program 14
- Coming up with Funding 15
- Recruitment 16
  - Campers 16
  - Adult Volunteers 16
- Evaluation and Follow-Up 18

Chapter 2: Preparation for Camp 19
- Applications 19
  - Campers 19
  - Peers 24
  - Adult Volunteers 25
- Pre-Camp Packet for Campers 30
  - Child Information 30
  - Parent Information 31
  - Miscellaneous Forms 32
- Finalizing the Details 33
  - Daily Schedule 33

T-Shirts....35
Camper Files....35
Grouping Campers....36
Gathering Materials and Creating Visuals....36
Visual Supports....36
Cabin Supplies....39
Campwide Supplies....40
Volunteer and Peer Training....41
Adult Volunteers....42
Peers....43

Chapter 3: The Camp Experience....45
Overall Management....45
Opening of Camp....49
Greeting and Arrival....49
Registration Table....49
Finding and Settling in the Cabin....50
Programming....51
Wake-Up and Breakfast Routine....52
Daily Activities....52
Types of Daytime Activities....52
Evening Activities....56

Chapter 4: Closing of Camp....59
Final Wrap-Up....60

Appendix....63
A – Group Activities....64
B – List of Games....73
C – Additional Resources....74

Preface

Summer camp can be a wonderful experience and should be made available to all children. Getting away from home and the typical routine and living in a more rustic setting, making new friends, roughing it a little, discovering new talents and abilities or honing existing ones – all can make children more self-reliant and better adjusted.

Over the course of my life, I have been a part of ten different camp programs for a variety of participants – as a camper, volunteer, or in administrative roles. From these different vantage points, it has been a joy to watch children and their families thrive in a camp setting, relaxing, releasing and enjoying themselves. Children with autism spectrum disorders are no different.

Pulling from these various experiences as well as my professional background, this book is written for educators, parents, service providers – anyone who is interested in camp and children with autism spectrum disorders. The book outlines the process for establishing a camp from the very first step through each stage of development, culminating in the actual camp experience, and finally the close of camp.

I wish you the best as you begin the journey of creating a camp geared to the specific needs of children with autism spectrum disorders. The camp you create will not be like anyone else's. It will be unique to your style and personality and, most important, to the needs of your campers. This book outlines a procedure to get the process going, serving as a springboard for your ideas for how to create the best possible summer experience for your campers. Enjoy the planning process and have fun with the programming.

In a well-supported environment based on careful planning, children will thrive and return home more confident and resilient, anxious to return to camp year after year.

– Jill Hudson

Foreword

Over the years I have worn a variety of hats related to my work in the field of autism spectrum disorders (ASD). Wearing one of these hats, I was once a camp director. My role as a camp director began in response to the concerns of parents of children on the spectrum. Many children had been asked to leave a summer camp due to an unsuccessful attempt to integrate them into a regular camp with neurotypical children. Along with a colleague I applied for a grant to start a camp for children with ASD. I was both excited and nervous when we were approved for the grant. I was excited at the prospect of the opportunities this would provide for the children. I was nervous because now I actually had to do it – I had to create a camp for children with ASD.

During our first couple of years, we climbed a steep learning curve. We learned by making a few mistakes, but mostly we learned from the children and their parents. We learned what worked and what didn't work; what the children needed and, most important, what they enjoyed. Since the first year we have made great strides in creating a well-rounded camp for children with ASD.

Children have come to our camps from all corners of the globe; we've had children come from as far away as Japan. But the real measure of success is whether or not children return year after year. The good news is that children who attend our camps return each year more excited than the year before. The camp allows them the chance to experience all the social interaction that other camps offer, but in a safe and supportive environment that fosters success. We give them the tools to develop their social identity and have fun while doing it.

Many of these children are meeting kids like themselves for the first time and are developing their very first friendships. It's amazing to see the transformation many of them undergo in just a week's time. Our counselors are the ones who make that happen, and none of them did it better than Jill Hudson.

Jill was one of the many graduate students who worked as counselors at our camps in the Kansas City area. Her amazing skills – her creativity, organizational skills and consummate desire to always work for the best interest of the children – make her the perfect person to write this guide on how to start a camp for children on the spectrum.

It's rare that you have students who teach you just as much, if not more, as you have taught them, but that is definitely the case when it comes to Jill Hudson. She is a unique woman with talents and skills that have made for a comprehensive and enlightened guide on creating camps for children with ASD.

– Brenda Smith Myles, Ph.D., is an associate professor at the University of Kansas, who writes and speaks internationally on Asperger Syndrome and autism

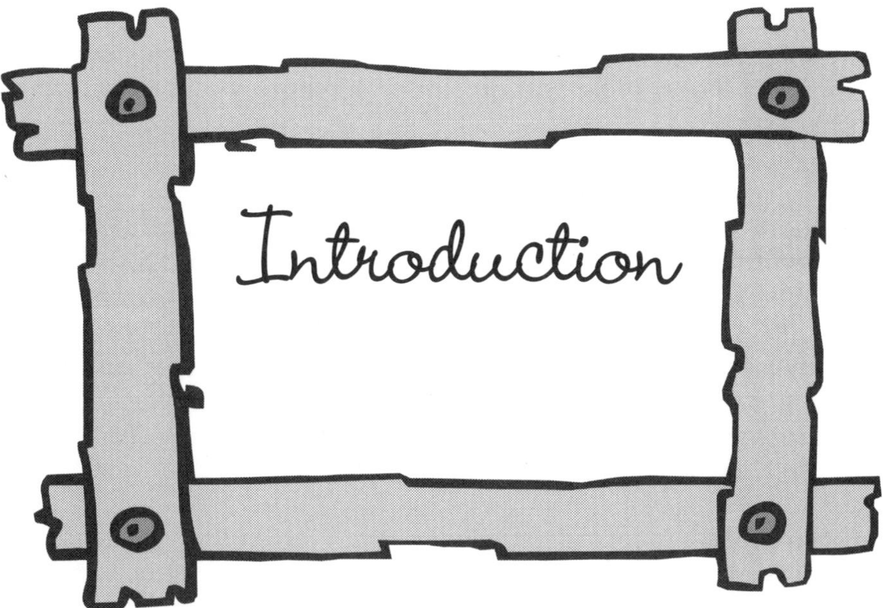

The anticipation of summer is a long-standing tradition for most school children. Knowing that school will be out for at least six weeks, freedom is within reach. Months before the final bell rings, children start counting the days, hours, even minutes. They are full of ideas for adventures and experiences for warm summer days. For many, one such adventure is summer camp.

Going to camp is something that many children look forward to with great excitement year after year. The opportunity to get away from home, daily routines, and everyday circumstances thrills and refreshes them. Camp is a time and place where children can relax and enjoy themselves, engaging in activities that are unique to the camp setting, such as horse back riding, archery or canoeing. Often children meet camper friends, children of their own age and with the same interests, who return to camp year after year.

A child's job is play. Play is how children express themselves, communicate, learn to handle new, often stressful, situations and cope with everyday life away from the vigilant eyes of their parents. It is their break. Away from the routine of everyday life and the monotony of the rule-bound day, children thrive in camp settings, making friendships and learning skills that last a lifetime.

Value of Camp for Children with Autism Spectrum Disorders

For children with autism spectrum disorders (ASD), camp is no less of a wonderful opportunity and experience, provided it is planned specifically to accommodate their needs. And that's where this book comes in. Before we get down to the nitty-gritty of planning and program development, let's take a quick look at the unique challenges that must be taken into consideration when setting up a camp for children with ASD.

ASD cover a range of diagnoses from mild to severe, including autism, pervasive developmental disorder– not otherwise specified (PDD-NOS), and Asperger Syndrome. Typically, children with ASD are characterized by a deficit in an overlapping triad of challenges related to (a) communication, (b) social interaction and (c) repetitive, idiosyncratic behaviors and/or special interests. Depending on the individual child, the range and combination of these characteristics vary, necessitating an individualized approach. In addition to these foundational characteristics, children with ASD typically have sensitive sensory systems, impairments in motor skills, and deficits in perception and relating to the environment around them.

Social Skills

Children and youth with ASD often lack the ability to understand themselves and may not be aware of what they do well or the areas in which they need assistance. Many struggle to develop and maintain friendships as well as to simply converse with others because they often lack the ability to perceive others' reactions, due to difficulty detecting facial cues, body language, feelings, intentions or inferences that others make. A social interaction is a constant give-and-take between those involved. Timing as well as reciprocal understanding is needed in order to actively participate. All of these areas present challenges to individuals on the autism spectrum.

Communication Skills

Communication skills, another of the triad of major characteristics, vary widely among children with ASD. Some children need to use pictures in order to indicate a preference or make a choice, whereas others have an advanced vocabulary, often appearing adult-like. Some children speak with scripts, repeating lines they have heard before, and some use repetitive speech patterns to get a point across. These children often speak out of context, or make delayed or off-topic responses to express a want or need.

Repetitive, Idiosyncratic Behaviors and Special Interests

Children with ASD prefer routine and repetition and often perform best in a predictable, structured environment. The ability to anticipate transition or change (facilitated by use of visual schedules, Social Stories™, Power Cards, etc.) alleviates the stress and anxiety that otherwise come from an unpredictable environment. They engage in idiosyncratic behaviors such as repeating scripts, using the same routine to get ready each morning or a ritual created before eating lunch. Overall, these interests and repetitious behaviors create a safe paradigm in which children with ASD function.

In addition, these children often have a special interest about which they know intricate facts, dates and trivia. Special interests vary from a love of vacuum cleaners to maps to movies. Their special interests drive their conversations, topics of study and behaviors.

James loved cats. He knew endless facts and figures about them and even acted like a cat at times. When he encountered a situation that was pleasant or pleasing to him, he purred softly. However, when he became overwhelmed or frustrated, he hissed and meowed aggressively at the infringing party.

When James arrived at camp, he used his cat-like senses to choose his bunk, sitting on each one until finally he began purring, claiming his bed. When James made his name sign for his bed, even the letters were made with cat-like drawings.

Sensory System

Many children with ASD have acute sensory systems; that is, they are sensitive to stimuli in the world around them. Further, they often do not perceive or process their environmental influences at the same rate as their peers. Walking into a crowded cafeteria with lots of children screaming or laughing can be overwhelming. Not having enough personal space while working on an art activity could inhibit their performance or eventually generate a meltdown. In the same way, not having enough visual reference when given a complex direction, or adequate supports to balance themselves while interacting in a physical activity, could cause the child to misunderstand a situation or not detect the sensory cues being given.

Children with ASD need assistance perceiving sensory stimuli as well as regulating their experiences. Some children use sensory input to regain inner stability when they feel overwhelmed, frustrated, nervous or scared. Many times, children want to pace, swing or squeeze a soft, squishy ball. The predictability and stability of a sensory intervention, such as that of a Slinky™ moving steadily back and forth, calms them and allows them to regain steadiness and control. In other instances they may have to be removed from the situation.

Motor Skills

Both fine- and gross-motor skills can be affected in children with ASD, inhibiting coordination, dexterity, balance and overall functioning. For example, many children have difficulty in timing, imitating and executing motor skills, and therefore may appear to be clumsy or awkward. However, with supports in place, such as visual boundaries outlined or the use of a light or a sound to signify movement to the next step, they are able to participate in physical motor activities as well as activities that require precision and joint coordination of skills.

Perception and Relating to the Environment

Many children with ASD remain in a heightened state of anxiety and a high level of stress most of the time. Though the signs may not be outward or detectable until the child has reached an extreme, he is almost constantly fending off the world, struggling to understand why others are laughing at a joke that doesn't seem funny, focusing intensely on opening his locker, made uncomfortable by the mass of bodies in the hallway bumping into him and moving around loudly as classes change, or being distracted in class when a light constantly is flickering.

All of these situations potentially bring stress because these children have to expend so much energy sorting and filtering the world around them. Due to some of their idiosyncratic behaviors, and because they are prone to overload or become outwardly stressed, children with ASD are easy targets for bullying or being teased by peers. In addition, if coerced by peers in order to become their friend, they may succumb to peer pressure, and as a result, engage in otherwise unacceptable, or worse yet, dangerous behavior. If they do not eagerly participate, but merely absorb the bullying and teasing that occurs, they may feel rejected and withdraw or become aggressive, taking out their stress in more intense ways. Providing choices and giving campers information that they need prior to a situation will decrease the level of stress and anxiety.

Purpose of This Book

Summer camp can give children with ASD a place to be themselves and take a deep breath after what is often a stressful school year. When well designed, camp allows these children to interact with children like them, with similar interests and similar needs, in an atmosphere where they are accepted and liked for who they are. As a result, bonds are often formed that last way beyond the week of camp.

When planning a camp for children with ASD, it is important to encourage and reinforce the use of appropriate social and communication skills as well as areas of strengths in all aspects of life at camp. Working together in the cabin and in various activities, campers cooperate and learn team-building skills – focusing on common goals and collaborating to achieve them. They learn to respect others' space and personal items in the cabin, and in the dining hall they have opportunities to socialize with a larger group, talking about the adventures of the day over a meal. Stories are told, skits are performed, games are played, jokes are told. The environment is nurturing, and children are supported according to their needs to optimize this powerful experience.

Camp is not immune to the behaviors or characteristics typically manifested by children with ASD. However, when proper supports are put into place, camp can be an overwhelmingly positive experience. Figure 1 demonstrates how camp can support and encourage some of the common characteristics of children with ASD.

Figure 1: Ways Camp Can Support Children with ASD

Relation to Others and Social Interactions
- Work together during activities
- Share living space

Communication
- Converse with cabin mates
- Share meals together as a bridge to conversation
- Debrief as a cabin at the end of the day

Conflict Resolution
- Work together to make group decisions
- Supported when working through differing opinions
- Participate in group games that teach how to be a good winner and a good loser

Perception
- Realize they are not the only person at camp – many are affected by each choice made
- Wait on others to travel to activities together
- Build relationships with one another

Need for Routine
- Use portable visual schedules
- Learn a camp routine, veering away from the typical daily routine
- Function in a relaxed environment with flexibility within boundaries

Motor Skills

- Ropes course, archery, horses, swimming – many activities create challenge and encourage use of coordinated motor skills structured specifically to meet the unique needs of campers with ASD

Self-Esteem

- Build on each individual's strengths
- Encouraged in an environment that does not tolerate bullying
- Relaxed atmosphere allowing campers to be themselves

Sensory Issues

- Introduced to many new sights, sounds, smells and textures
- Given freedom, opportunity and time to explore new environment
- Participate in daily sensory fun activity as a release, such as a shaving cream fling

This book will discuss how to create a camp program, plan for and successfully run a camp for children with ASD, including vital information to consider while preparing each aspect of camp. In addition, it will give insight into much-needed supports that maximize children's experiences and make camp an environment in which children with ASD will flourish.

CHAPTER 1
Creating a Camp Plan

Children with ASD need an outlet in the summer where they can let down, run and play. Camp can provide such an environment if activities are structured and supported for success. Creating a camp begins with the hint of an idea and a willingness to follow through. It can be conceptualized and started by anyone with an interest in children with ASD – parents, educators, service providers, and so on.

An important first step is to develop a philosophy and purpose that reflect the mission and objectives for the camp. These statements in turn frame the policies, procedures and program that will be implemented during the camp experience. Such common ground is also necessary when recruiting others to make up the leadership team, looking for counselors, and determining a target population of campers. Also, when communicating the needs of camp to potential donors and supporters, a detailed and well-stated purpose, philosophy and plan will more fully convey the mission and purpose of camp and better express the areas where contributions will benefit.

Figure 2 lists the key areas that should be thought through when developing a camp plan. Each of these areas is further explained in the following.

Figure 2: Key Concepts for Conceptualizing and Developing a Camp Plan

- Determining the Concept
- Choosing a Facility
- Developing a Program
- Recruiting Campers
- Sharing the Vision
- Developing Policy
- Coming up with Funding
- Conducting Evaluation and Follow-Up

Determining the Concept

The first planning decision involves determining whether the camp will be created as an independent experience at a campground where the program is not already outlined or predetermined for campers, or whether it will take place within a pre-existing camp for all children, but adapted to meet the unique needs of children with ASD. These two basic types of camps are planned somewhat differently in terms of overall management and coordination, and each has definite advantages and disadvantages.

My personal preference is to find a pre-existing camp where our group is the only one for the specified period. That allows the group to bring in its own program and activities and gives the leadership team freedom in planning and scheduling. Nevertheless, the leadership team must coordinate with the directors of the camp, identifying and clarifying the adaptations necessary to support the success of campers with ASD.

Along with the decision to merge into a functioning camp or create a program independently, a mission statement should be created as well as objectives for hosting or adapting a camp. These issues will be further outlined in the following.

Sharing the Vision

Determining who will be a part of the leadership team is a crucial step. This team makes decisions that affect all aspects of camp, including planning, management, programming and facilitating/supporting campers. In most cases, the majority of the members on the leadership team are volunteers.

Leadership Team

When looking around for members, select individuals who are like-minded in purpose and performance, as team members must be able to work well together for many hours at a time and under a variety of circumstances. While it is imperative that the team work as a unit and progress in the same direction at the same pace, it is also important to evaluate the skills of each and make sure member skills complement each other, thereby covering all the various facets that go into planning and running a successful camp. If everyone has ideas for programming, but no one is capable of or wants to assume administrative leadership, for example, the team is out of balance.

After careful thought has been given to who should be a part of the leadership team, the camp plan should be presented to them in a clear, concise manner to ensure that each member understands the philosophy, purpose and direction of camp, and is able or willing to go along.

To assist the leadership team in areas where they may lack sufficient experience and knowledge, a variety of members from the community may be consulted for their expertise. This may include a professional fund-raiser who knows how to tap into local businesses and organizations for support, or a marketing director who knows how best to promote camp and recruit volunteers. In other words, the leadership team does not have to do or know everything about planning a camp, but it must be resourceful and willing to facilitate the process and seek out and manage those who agree to contribute talent and/or money.

Timeline

A timeline should be created to outline and prioritize the items and activities that will require planning and attention. A general plan can be developed, listing those items that must be secured first, such as finding a facility and setting the dates of camp. The amount of time between the decision to create a camp and the actual camp dates will determine the framework within which camp must be planned.

While as little time as four months has produced a fine camp, a full year may be necessary to plan out and carefully and deliberately attend to the myriad details of a successful camp. Time should be allotted in the process if external funding is needed. Some grantors require that proposals and applications be submitted up to a year in advance. Further, recruitment of both campers and volunteers should start no later than three or four months prior to camp. For volunteers this allows time to gather and process applications, review references, obtain background checks, and facilitate volunteer training. For campers, this allows time to gather and process applications and secure a health check, parental permission and all other relevant information.

In addition, in terms of the program, many resources will need to be confirmed over the months prior to camp such as securing entertainers for evening events, whereas other details will be attended to the week before camp such as gathering all the necessary materials and supplies, packing them and transporting them to the camp facility. By creating a timeline, all details of camp are written out and prioritized for the leadership team to oversee, allowing individual team members to take responsibility or delegate the individual tasks. Figure 3 lists a sample timeline divided into month blocks.

Figure 3: Sample Timeline

1 year-9 months
- Develop a plan and philosophy
- Develop policies
- Set camp dates
- Find potential locations
- Submit grants
- Secure insurance
- Recruit leadership team

9-6 months
- Secure a facility
- Develop program details
- Contact potential donors
- Locate entertainers
- Develop applications

6-4 months
- Advertise for campers
- Recruit volunteers
- Confirm entertainers

4 months-2 months
- Accept applications
- Send out pre-camp packets
- Process volunteer information and conduct background checks
- Hold a fund-raising event

2 months-1 month
- Gather all materials
- Create visuals
- Order t-shirts
- Divide cabin groups
- Create daily schedules

Weeks prior
- Hold volunteer orientation
- Inventory and pack materials
- Transport all materials to camp

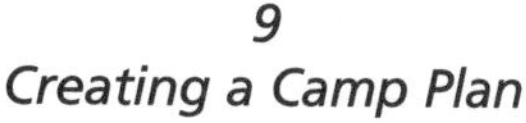

Choosing a Facility

Location and Physical Layout

Determining the location of the camp is one of the most pivotal details. Figure 4 outlines what to look for when considering a camp facility. The site should be conveniently located and easily accessible. If children will be coming from all over a state or large geographic area, the campground should be located relatively close to an airport and major highways.

The area of the campground should be large enough to accommodate the number of campers and counselors who will participate. As a general rule, for children with ASD, there should be an almost equal number of staff to campers, possibly a 1-to-2 or 2-to-3 ratio. Counselors are not attached specifically to campers, but paired to provide the necessary individualized support and allow for one camper to take a break while others still participate. In some cases, a child will need 1-to-1 support; this will increase the number of volunteers needed.

Figure 4: Considerations When Choosing a Camp Facility

- ☐ Convenient location
- ☐ Accessible to major highways
- ☐ Cabins
  - ☐ With attached restrooms
  - ☐ Air-conditioned or fans
  - ☐ Outlets available
  - ☐ With meeting room
  - ☐ With capacity for campers and counselors
- ☐ Amenities for evening events
  - ☐ Hayride
  - ☐ Campfire
  - ☐ Extended hours in the pool
  - ☐ Large area for group gathering (a field or covered space)
- ☐ Activities available
  - ☐ Swimming pool or lake
  - ☐ Horses
  - ☐ Ropes course
  - ☐ Canoeing
  - ☐ Fishing
- ☐ Simple campground layout
- ☐ Short travel distances between activities, cabins, cafeteria, etc.
- ☐ Sharing camp facility with another group or renting alone
- ☐ Willing to accommodate food issues and special diets in the cafeteria
- ☐ Allows mixed-gender counselors/ campers in cabins
- ☐ Willingness to adapt and accommodate unique needs of the children
- ☐ Other:

Overcrowding cabins will cause spatial issues, which can be particularly challenging for children with ASD due to their sensory issues. Depending on the size of the cabins, it is recommended that cabins not be filled to capacity but at a maximum of three-fourths full to allow the space that will be needed for the campers.

Take into consideration whether the cabins have restrooms, which provides convenience, or if campers will have to travel to find facilities. Depending on the geographic location in which the camp is being established and the time of year when it will be held, the issue of providing campers with a cool space will also need to be a high consideration. Inquire whether the cabins have an air conditioner or fans only. In addition, question if outlets are available for campers to plug in their personal fans if desired. Some cabins have a central meeting space that is separate from the bunk area, which can be used for activi-

ties or a place to connect a television to show movies for relaxation, for example. Determine the exact nature and layout of the camp so details can be assessed to best fit the need.

The campground should be laid out in a way that reduces the travel time between activities. Areas such as the cabins, the cafeteria/dining hall, the pool, the playground, and the spaces used for activities should be in close proximity. This allows the day to flow without wasting a lot of time traveling back and forth instead of being actively engaged in activities. If given the choice by the camp facility, choose cabins in a central location. Figure 5 displays an air view of a camp facility.

Figure 5: Air View of Camp Facility

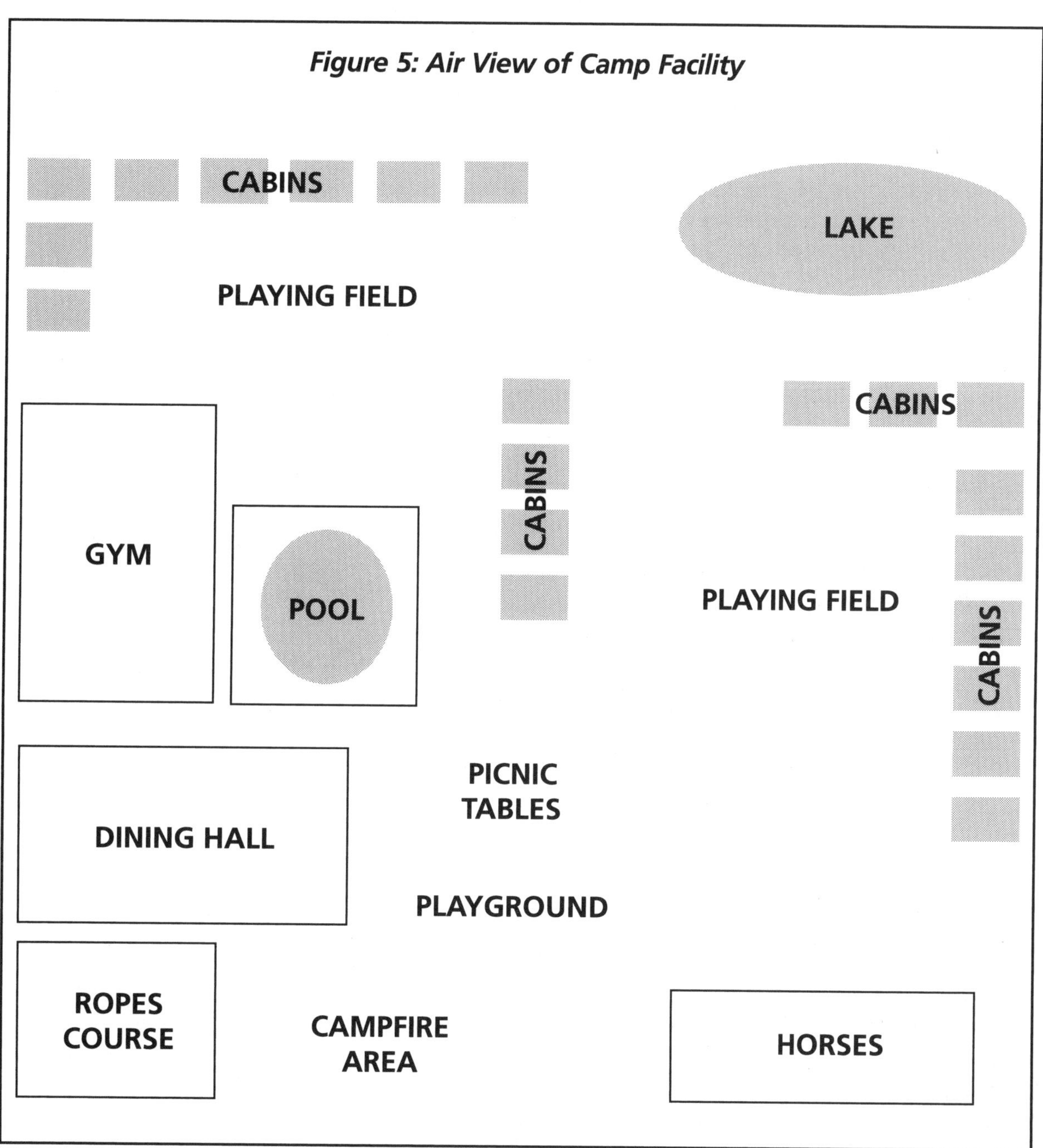

Program – Activities

Depending on the program outlined in the camp plan, a campground may be chosen that has an existing program that can be adapted for campers with ASD. If so, it is important to know if other children will be at the campground at the same time. If the camp plan specifies creating a program uniquely for the children with ASD, determine whether a given camp will support the details of that program, such as whether it has a swimming pool or a lake nearby. Also, take into account what type of evening activities are offered, such as a hayride or campfire, and whether a large room is available for group activities. Some campgrounds charge extra for special amenities, whereas others include them in the overall cost. Therefore, when considering the cost of comparable camp facilities, be sure to check this out. Chapter 3 presents more details and programming activities.

Campground Staff

In addition to the physical aspects of a campground, personnel should be evaluated as well. Most established campgrounds have hired staff that will be present during the camps. When discussing your campers and the intended program, be clear about the unique needs of the children and the visual, social and physical adaptations they require. Letting the staff know these details up-front and communicating with them about the importance of their role during camp will open the door for a great working relationship and a happier camp experience for the children.

A brief overview of the characteristics and needs of children with ASD can be offered to the staff before camp begins, allowing them to understand that they will have to be flexible and adaptable with the campers. For example, cooks in the kitchen may face food issues, including requests for special diets; therefore, alternate food may have to be prepared that some campers will bring from home, such as for Sam, who must have one strawberry pop-tart for breakfast each morning, or Charles who is on a restricted glutein-free diet and brings alternate meals that need to be warmed.

one 1	Wait in line
two 2	Get your food
three 3	Find your seat
four 4	Eat
five 5	Put dishes away

Visuals will need to be hung as reminders to campers about the schedule, protocol or details of activities. Directions may need to be explained in more detail and, in general, communicating with the campers may look different than what the staff is generally used to, such as using a story strip to review the procedure for dining in the cafeteria.

Safety is also a concern as children, such as Chuck, may want to return to the barn to see the horses during unscheduled hours, or Marcus, who likes to swim in the deep end while other campers are jumping off the diving board. When the staff better understand the needs of children with ASD, they are more accommodating of the necessary adjustments.

Mixed-Gender Cabins

One additional consideration to discuss with the camp administrator is the policy on mixed-gender cabins. As a general rule, all campers should be divided among boy cabins and girl cabins. However, depending on the ratio of campers to volunteers, often there are not enough male counselors to cover the male campers. In this case, match female counselors with the youngest male campers.

Not all camp facilities allow mixing of genders within cabins. Knowing the estimated ratio of campers and counselors who will be participating will assist in the assignment of each within a cabin. Choosing a facility that understands this challenge allows for freedom when planning and recruiting counselors. If a camp site does not allow for mixed-gender cabins, the number of campers participating must be reduced to stay in proportion to the number of counselors of the appropriate sex.

Developing a Policy

Creating policies helps support standard procedures as well as emergency situations that can occur. For example, policies can be created for routine procedures such as arrival to camp and how to carry out the various programs throughout the week. Policies should also be defined for the what-ifs of camp – those instances that are not planned for, but that often occur, such as bedwetting or a camper running off or being injured.

Setting policies will ensure that volunteers understand their individual role in an emergency, the appropriate protocol for contacting a member of the leadership team, when necessary, filling out paperwork, and so on. By planning a response system and educating all volunteers on the procedures, incidents can be remedied with little disruption to the regular routine of the other campers, and the safety of all is more likely to be preserved. Incident reports are further discussed in Chapter 3.

Chuck wandered off from the group while they were traveling to the pool. He wanted to pass by the horse barn again and say hello to the horses. When Maggie, Chuck's counselor, noticed that Chuck was headed for the barn, she used her walkie-talkie to call to the wranglers and the leadership team to let them know he was coming. Not until she received a response that they had spotted Chuck and were following him, did Maggie stop watching him and continue with her other campers. After Maggie had gotten her campers safely to the pool, she left them with the other counselors and then headed toward the barn to meet Chuck.

Chuck was slowly walking towards the barn, giddy that he was about to see the horses again. Jack, a member of the leadership team, met him on the way and thwarted the plan, reminding him of the rules and encouraging him to return to his group. The dangers of wandering off were explained as well as the importance of staying with the group or at least a counselor. In addition, Maggie used Chuck's interest in horses to develop a game that she and Chuck could play together. Chuck could ride on her back like a horse, or walk in front of her with her hands on his shoulders while he steered the horse via the imaginary reins. Soon many of the boys in the cabin wanted to make a train with Maggie and Chuck. Chuck was in front steering, and several campers lined up in the back like a train. Maggie was able to keep all of her campers together because they were all attached to her!

Sally was prone to bedwetting, so her mother had noted this in the application materials and had packed two sets of sheets. However, Sally was embarrassed when she woke up the first morning of camp in a wet bed. Emma, Sally's counselor, was aware that this might occur and after the campers left for their first activity, she returned to the cabin to strip the bed and remake it with the dry sheets. Emma then took the wet sheets to be washed and dried and picked them up in the afternoon, returning them to Sally's bag while the campers were at the pool. The entire situation was taken care of without any of the campers knowing that Sally had wet her bed.

Policies may also be created to establish parameters for recruiting campers, for preparing for camp, for fund-raising, for evaluation procedures and for follow-up with campers. Anything that is an established process should be put into print and disseminated to the relevant parties to best communicate expectations and allow all participants to see and work toward the common goal – a fun, enriching and safe camp experience.

Insurance

One legal issue and safety precaution to consider while planning camp is to find insurance coverage. A general liability insurance plan should be established as blanket coverage for both campers and volunteer staff. This protects the group establishing camp in case of an accident or injury while the children are at camp. Major insurance companies offer standard coverage, depending on the size, location and activities provided at camp. Some campgrounds have an already existing insurance plan to which their campers must subscribe. Whether it comes from the camp or from an outside source, having a general liability coverage plan is imperative.

Developing the Program

After evaluating the resources available at the campground, program planning for the campers can begin. If the campsite has an already existing program in which children with ASD will participate, adaptations should be thought through and implemented for each activity so that the campers are supported for success. If a campwide program does not exist, the leadership team will be able to develop one specifically designed for the children participating.

A schedule should be outlined in general terms, including daily activities, morning and evening routines within the cabin, meals throughout the day, and a list of potential special evening events. By providing a sketch of activities and events, further planning can move forward in more detail, such as budgeting and recruiting volunteers. Programming will be discussed in detail in Chapter 3.

Coming up with Funding

Setting a budget for camp is a crucial element that needs careful attention. It is important to make camp affordable while at the same time making sure that everything is covered. The cost per camper as well as per volunteer should be absorbed into the overall cost of camp so that volunteers are not paying to participate. Determining what funding is available out of a general operating budget (e.g., based on camp registration fees) will help set a guideline for overall spending and determine what funds may need to be raised in contributions from outside sources.

The leadership team manages the overall financial planning and budgeting, but fund-raising and soliciting contributions is often best delegated to a specialized volunteer team. If camp is covered under a 501(c) 3 non-profit organization, such as a school or church, donations can be made as a tax deduction, making them more attractive to potential donors. Even if camp is not covered under this tax code, corporations and local donors are often willing to sponsor parts of the camp's expenses. (Non-profit status typically takes about a year to establish, so start early. Consult an attorney for assistance with establishing 501(c) 3 status.)

When preparing to approach potential donors, it is a good idea to make up a form that divides costs among the varied activities of camp so they can more easily pick the specific event(s) they want to sponsor. For example, the Tuesday night carnival might be underwritten by Jones Insurance, whereas the Wednesday night hayride and square dance may be sponsored by Joe Dee's School Supplies. Other donors may want to make in-kind contributions such as t-shirts or supplies for the art activities. In addition, contributions can be made to a general scholarship fund to support children who would like to come to camp, but cannot afford to pay the full price.

Figure 6 provides a sample budget based on 100 campers and 75 volunteers.

Figure 6: Sample Camp Budget

Item	Cost
Marketing/advertising	$300
Postage/copying	$250
Facility	$21,250
Insurance coverage	$1,000
T-shirts	$650
Special events	
Western Night	$100
Carnival	$1,000
Mission Impossible	$100
Movie Night	$20
Cabin supplies	$500
General supplies	$500
Visual supports	$100
Art activities – four days	$300
Sensory fun – four days	$150
Miscellaneous expenses	$300
Compensatory expenses for leadership team	$300
Staff training	$100
TOTAL	**$26,920**

Price per camper (total divided by 100 – to cover cost of volunteers) **$269.20**

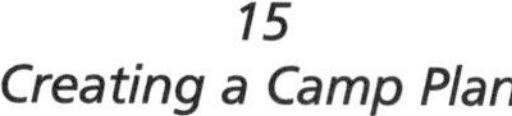

Recruitment

Under the heading of recruitment, plan on at least two types: recruitment of children to participate in the camp and recruitment of volunteers to help support and facilitate the campers.

Campers

It is recommended that campers be at least seven years old in order to participate in an overnight camp. This age restriction has generally been found to ease the transition of being away from home and foster a willingness to participate in the various camp activities. Some camps allow children to remain campers until age 18 or 19, whereas others create positions for junior counselors when children reach this age, if otherwise appropriate. This way they are still able to participate in camp, but are given more responsibility and see an administrative side to camp in addition to being campers. These junior counselors are typically paired with adult volunteers and assist in the younger cabins with activities. Junior counselors are included in volunteer training prior to camp to outline their role as assistants within the cabin. (Material for volunteer training is mentioned in Chapter 2.)

Besides children with ASD, some children attend camp as peer models. These children must also fall into the target age range, and may be friends or siblings of children with ASD. Peer models serve as examples and helpers in the cabins and throughout camp, thereby benefiting the other campers while learning leadership and other valuable skills themselves – besides having a good time. Once they arrive at camp, all peers will be gathered for a special meeting, giving them information about camp, their role within the cabin and how best to interact with fellow campers. (Training material is outlined at the end of Chapter 2.)

Information about camp can be distributed to families through schools, churches, doctor offices, service providers, local parent groups and other community organizations. A brief description of camp and important details such as the dates, cost and location should be given as well as a name and number to contact for more information or to request an application.

Adult Volunteers

Typically adults, college age or older, make up the camp volunteers. Some want to participate because they love camp and being with children. Others volunteer because they work directly or indirectly with children with ASD on a daily basis and want to work with them in a relaxed environment. Almost anyone who is willing to participate can be useful and help to make a successful week. It is important, however, to have a balance or abundance of those who are knowledgeable or have experience with children with ASD versus those who do not. Pair those who love camp, but are not as familiar with children with ASD, with volunteers who are comfortable and well experienced.

Volunteers may be recruited from a variety of sources. Good sources to begin with are those who routinely work directly with children with ASD, including educators, speech-language pathologists, physical and occupational therapists and other service providers. In addition, those who are in training for these types of positions gain a great deal of knowledge and hands-on experience from participating in camp. Contacting local professors and developing a protocol that meets university requirements will create a partnership that allows students, undergraduate or graduate, to gain field experience credit from volunteering at camp. Therefore, local colleges or universities offer a wonderful bank of potential volunteers.

Recruiting from churches, civic groups, children's hospitals, and businesses extends awareness of children with ASD and provides opportunity for participation by those who may not otherwise encounter these children but want to contribute in meaningful ways.

Some parents also want to be a part of camp and are welcomed if they volunteer. However, typically, parents are not deliberately recruited as counselors for camp, allowing them a break while their child is gone. As a type of compromise, some parents may want to assist in the office prior to camp, assisting with gathering materials, organizing files or putting last-minute details together. This allows them to participate, but also provides a break while their child is at camp as they won't be attending on site.

Volunteer Application

Once the various volunteer roles have been identified, develop a volunteer application that includes a description of each position. (Volunteers will participate in training to review their role at camp, characteristics of children with ASD, the protocol for camp and how to support campers for a successful week.) Many volunteer positions are available, depending on the level of involvement that a volunteer is able to give. Figure 7 lists typical volunteer roles.

Figure 7: Typical Volunteer Roles

Leadership team – Oversees the details of camp and carries out managerial duties before, during and after camp

Cabin counselors – Take care of campers throughout camp; stay in cabins with campers and accompany them to all activities

Photographer/videographer – Videos week of camp; creates a memory video and slide show for parents; takes photographs of campers during activities throughout camp; not responsible for a group of campers

Nurse/medical personnel – Distribute medication to campers and care for all medical needs

Activity leaders – Facilitate daytime activity groups such as art, sensory activities, rhythm and movement, or fishing; not responsible for a group of campers

Evening event leaders – Coordinate and assist with special event details such as running a booth at the carnival or helping make s'mores at the campfire; typically volunteer for only one evening event

In addition to counselors, there is a need for nurses and other medical personnel who can distribute medication, small-group activity leaders, and a photographer. These volunteers are needed for the entire length of camp. Some volunteers may be recruited to help with a single activity such as an evening event, as mentioned above. Many businesses are interested in community service and are looking for a place to send a group of employees to offer volunteer services. Recruiting such groups for a large activity allows the camp counselors to remain with their campers instead of having to run evening activities.

Chapter 2 will return to recruitment of both campers and volunteers, specifically as it relates to the necessary screening, paperwork and training.

Evaluation and Follow-Up

As part of your planning, also put in place a way to evaluate the effectiveness of camp. Carefully review each aspect of the program, including development of the leadership team, recruitment of staff and campers, details of the facility chosen and the activities planned, camper arrival and departure procedures, fund-raising and sponsorships, and the overall efficiency of the plan. Upon completion of the camp, review and note the results of the evaluation, making adjustments and changes to benefit future camps. An example evaluation form is included in Chapter 4.

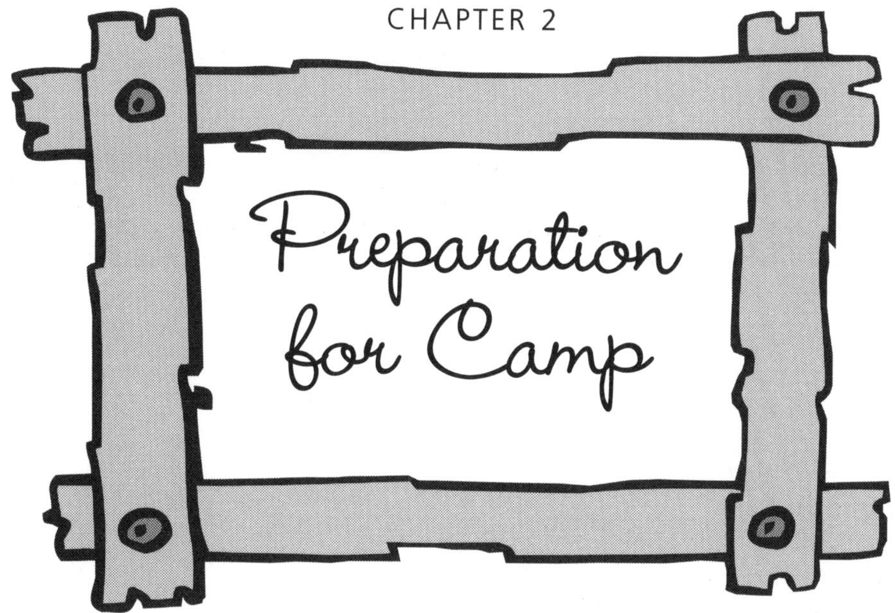
CHAPTER 2
Preparation for Camp

Once a basic plan is in place, more detailed preparations can begin. According to the timeline, general camp information must be distributed and recruitment initiated as outlined in Chapter 1. Once you have a general idea of the number and type of campers who will be attending, fine-tuning of activities and confirmation of evening events can proceed, which in turn allows for supplies to be gathered and allotted. Pre-camp preparations are mostly administrative. When well planned and executed, they produce a great week of camp.

Applications

Campers

The camp application affords an opportunity to gather information about the needs and strengths of each child. It subsequently allows for adaptations to be made and children to be adequately supported so that all will have a successful camp experience. When creating the camper application, make sure it is clear, concise and thorough. Once the forms have gone out, it's too late to add that forgotten item.

In addition to requesting detailed contact information, it is important to ask about the child's medical history, motivators and stress triggers, previous camp participation, and activities in which the child may need assistance, such as swimming or daily life functions. To be able to conserve routines and adaptations that are already in place for the child, ask about communication methods, what to do when the child has a meltdown and if a reward or work system exists. Figure 8 provides a sample camper application.

Once a completed camper application is received, date it to ensure a place is held for the camper and a waiting list can be created in case applications are received after the camper limit has been reached. Notify families as early as possible that their child has a place by sending a confirmation letter and a packet of information detailing what to pack for camp, when and where (include a map) to drop the child off for camp, general camp rules, a social narrative about camp and forms to be filled out, such as health forms (see pre-camp packet section page 30).

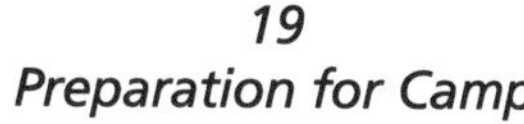

Figure 8: Camper Application

Name ______________________________ Gender ____________________

Address ____

____

Phone Number ________________ Date of Birth ______________ Age _____

School ____________________________ Grade Completing ______________

Medical Diagnosis ____

Current Medications ____

Allergies ____

Other Medical Considerations ____

Special Diet ____

Names and Ages of Siblings Who Will Also Be Participating ______________

____

____

____

Emergency Contact Information

Name ____

Phone Number ______________________ Relation ______________________

Name ____

Phone Number ______________________ Relation ______________________

Please describe your child's needs and existing accommodations for each:

- Communication style and system:

- Social interactions:

- Stress triggers:

- Repetitive behaviors and special interests:

- Behavior management techniques used:

- Calming activities:

- Motivators:

- Interests:

- Strengths:

- Work/reward system:

- Typical morning routine:

- Typical bedtime routine:

If you answer YES to any question below, please explain.

Has your child spent the night away from home before?	YES	NO
Has your child attended camp before?	YES	NO
Does your child need one-on-one support?	YES	NO
Does your child need assistance swimming?	YES	NO
Does your child need assistance toileting?	YES	NO
Does your child need assistance eating?	YES	NO
Does your child sleep through the night?	YES	NO

Is your child a runner? YES NO

Does your child wear any assistive devices? YES NO
(glasses, retainer, etc.)

If yes, please list.

Please list any additional comments you would like to share with our staff about your child:

Child t-shirt size: Small____ Medium_____ Large_____ X-Large____

NOTE: We cannot process your application unless signed and accompanied by a deposit.

My child has permission to attend *(Camp name here)* summer 2006. I understand that as a participant, my child may be photographed or videotaped during activities and that these photographs/video clips may be used in the future at the discretion of (*Camp name)*. There will be no financial compensation for use or publication of these photographs/videos. I understand that (*Camp name)* cannot be responsible for lost or broken items and that all personal items brought to camp must be claimed at the end of each session or they may be given away at the end of the summer. I understand and will comply with the schedule and policies of (*Camp name)*. I understand that a $100 non-refundable deposit must accompany this application in order to hold my child's place. The remaining balance will be paid in full on or prior to the first day of day camp.

Signature ____ Date ____________________

Check the session your child will be attending:

____ June 6-10
____ June 13-17
____ July 11-15
____ July 18-22

Peers

Peer models are a wonderful addition to camp. They are able to assist the campers in the cabin and demonstrate skills that the campers can mirror. Typically, peer models are friends or siblings of campers with ASD and are, therefore, comfortable and familiar with at least one camper. Although peer models are a welcomed part of camp, they should be limited in number to provide space for children with ASD who desire a camp experience. Not all camps include peer models, preferring to hold 100% capacity for children with ASD. This is a choice the leadership team must make early on.

If peers are a part of camp, develop a separate application form to gain a better understanding of the child's desire to participate. Not only does this allow the peer to reflect on her role at camp, it also informs the leadership team to better match peers with children with ASD. Peers are also campers and should enjoy their time at camp. They serve as examples and helpers, but should not be overwhelmed with responsibility.

Miguel had participated at school in a lunch bunch with Sam, his friend who has Asperger Syndrome. He heard about an opportunity to go to summer camp with him as a peer buddy and decided he would like to try it. Miguel was able to use his experience at school to assist Sam. While at breakfast at camp, Miguel brought up topics of conversation such as Star Wars that he knew Sam liked to talk about. Miguel was able to ask questions and facilitate a conversation with all the boys at the table. When they were done eating, Miguel helped the boys remember to clear their place at the table and pointed them in the right direction to drop off their used dishes.

In addition to a completed application form, ask for two or three letters of reference from teachers, neighbors, or camp or youth leaders who have witnessed the applicant's character and behavior around children with special needs. Figure 9 gives an example of forms for peer models.

Figure 9: Questions to Include in Peer Model Application

Why do you want to be a peer model at camp?

When and how have you interacted with children with disabilities?

What do you expect camp to be like?

Please describe your previous experiences at camp.

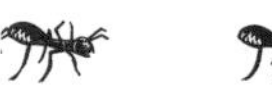

Peer Reference Form

Name of reference ______________________________

Address ______________________________

Phone number ______________________________

Name of Peer ______________________________

Relation to the child ______________________ Years known __________

In the space below, briefly describe the child's character qualities, relationship to other children, and why you think he/she would be a good peer model to children with disabilities.

Adult Volunteers

An application should also be created for the adult volunteers. Because some volunteers simply love camp and others volunteer because they love children with ASD, be sure to gather information in both areas to create a balance of what skills and background volunteers bring to the camp experience (see Figure 10 for a sample). Clearly explain each volunteer position with a place for the applicant to indicate his or her preference. Include questions about overall previous camp experience, as well as detailed information on specific aspects of camp such as comfort level assisting with crafts, games, horses, swimming, and so on.

If possible, give volunteers a preference of age group and, where needed, gender (often there are more male campers but more female counselors). Finally, ask each volunteer to list two to three references to verify his or her character and integrity.

Figure 10: Adult Volunteer Application

Name ______________________ Gender ______________

Address ____

____

Email Address ___________________________________

Phone Number ____________ Date of Birth __________ Age ___

SS# ________ Driver's License Information: State ____ Number ________

Name of person who referred you to the camp or how you found out about this camp ____

Current Occupation

Position ____

Description _____________________________________

Contact Information ______________________________

Educational Background

High school _____________________________________

Undergraduate institution __________________________

Major ______________________ Year of graduation ________

Additional training or graduate work:

Area of emphasis _________________________________

Year completed ___________________________________

Briefly explain your previous camp experiences _______________

____

____

____

Briefly explain your experience or training for working with children ____________

____

____

Briefly describe your involvement with children with special needs ____________

____

____

Briefly describe areas of additional volunteer work ____________________________

____

____

____

Please list any special skills that enhance your work with children with autism spectrum disorders ____

____

Describe your goals and expectations for being a volunteer at this camp ________

____

____

Have you ever been arrested or convicted of a felony? YES NO
If yes, briefly explain ____

____

____

Have you ever been fired or asked to leave a job, or suspended or expelled from school? YES NO If yes, briefly explain ________________________________

____

____

Available Volunteer Positions

Cabin counselors
Caretakers of campers throughout camp; stay in cabins with campers and accompany them to all activities

Videographer
Videos week of camp; creates a memory video and slide show for parents; not responsible for a group of campers

Photographer
Takes photographs of campers during activities throughout camp; not responsible for a group of campers

Nurse/medical personnel
Distribute medication to campers and care for all medical needs

Activity leaders
Facilitate daytime activity groups such as art, sensory, rhythm and movement, or fishing; not responsible for a group of campers

Evening event leaders
Coordinate or assist with special event details such as running a booth at the carnival or helping make s'mores at the campfire; typically volunteer for only one evening event

Position Applying for:

☐ Cabin counselor
☐ Nurse/medical personnel
☐ Photographer
☐ Videographer
☐ Activity leader Please indicate which activity ____________________________

Preference of Camper:

☐ Male ☐ Female
☐ Age 7-8 ☐ Age 9-11 ☐ Age 12-14 ☐ Age 15-17

Please indicate if you have a special skill or training in a specific area. Check all that apply:

☐ CPR ☐ Musical instrument (please specify) ☐ Sign language

☐ First aid ☐ Singing ☐ Spanish

☐ Sport (please specify)____________________________

☐ Other ____________________________

T-shirt size: ☐ Small ☐ Medium ☐ Large ☐ X-Large

Name of physician ______________________________

Please list any health-related limitations ______________________________

____

Emergency Contact Information:

Name ______________________________

Phone Number ______________ Relation ______________

Personal References (please list three):

1. Name ______________________________

   Phone Number ______________________________

   Relationship ______________________________

2. Name ______________________________

   Phone Number ______________________________

   Relationship ______________________________

3. Name ______________________________

   Phone Number ______________________________

   Relationship ______________________________

I willingly submit the information on this application as current and correct. I consent to a criminal background check and the checking of my references. I understand that I am applying for a volunteer position, but am committed and fully willing to participate at each session for which I am accepted as a volunteer. I understand that as a participant, I may be photographed or videotaped during activities and that these photographs/video clips may be used in the future at the discretion of *(camp name)*. There will be no financial compensation for use or publication of these photographs/videos. I understand that (*camp name)* cannot be responsible for lost or broken items and that all personal items brought to camp must be claimed at the end of each session or they may be given away at the end of the summer. I understand and will comply with the schedule and policies of *(camp name)*. I am not, nor will I be, under the influence of any chemical substance (other than prescription medication) while at camp.

Signature ______________________________ Date ______________

Printed Name ______________________________

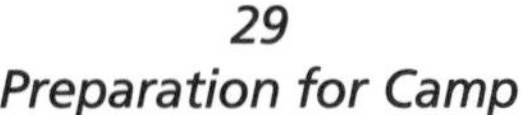

Once the applications have been received, conduct a careful screening to check backgrounds and references for each potential volunteer to ensure they will be a good match for camp. If the applicant works in an environment that involves children, he or she has probably been cleared through a criminal background check; if that's the case, consideration should be given to whether or not an additional check is necessary. For all others, arrange for a thorough background check. Consult your local police for information on this procedure as well as how long the process takes.

In addition, personal interviews with all viable applicants are recommended. This allows the leadership team to get to know the volunteer and obtain a better perspective of the applicant's personality, strengths and potential contributions to camp. Pair the counselors with more experience, both with camp and with children with ASD, with the volunteers who have less experience. This will balance out the cabins and best support the campers.

When a volunteer is accepted for camp, send a packet of information, including the position to which the applicant has been assigned, a health form, a sample camp schedule, information about volunteer training and suggested items to pack for camp. To signify acceptance of the invitation to participate in camp, have volunteers call somebody on the leadership team to confirm their participation and reserve a place for volunteer training. Figure 11 lists suggested items for counselor to pack for camp.

Figure 11: Items for Counselors to Pack

- ☐ Alarm clock
- ☐ Wrist watch
- ☐ Backpack
- ☐ Flashlight
- ☐ Costumes for special events (e.g., a cowboy hat, camouflage shirt)
- ☐ Shorts
- ☐ T-shirts
- ☐ Jeans or long pants
- ☐ Socks
- ☐ Underwear
- ☐ Tennis shoes
- ☐ Flip-flops or sandals
- ☐ Bathing suit
- ☐ Lightweight jacket or raincoat
- ☐ Sunscreen
- ☐ Bug repellent
- ☐ Bath towel
- ☐ Beach towel
- ☐ Toiletries
- ☐ Sleeping bag or sheets and blanket
- ☐ Pillow
- ☐ Laundry bag

Pre-Camp Packet for Campers

Once the camper has been accepted into camp, a packet of information should be sent to the camper's family. Sending information and expectations to the campers prior to their arrival at camp ensures a smoother transition and creates anticipation and, where appropriate, preparation for specific camp activities. This is beneficial to both the child and the parents and ensures a more successful camp experience for all.

Child Information

To prepare the child for camp, a Social Story™ (Gray, 1995) or social narrative may be written, outlining a variety of aspects for camp. Written in first person from the child's perspective, a Social Story™ tells about an upcoming event, predicts possible interactions and activities, and creates flexibility within a routine. It allows the reader to gain perspective and better anticipate a situation ahead of time.

A social narrative for camp could begin with getting ready for camp, moving into the arrival process and an overall view of what will occur during the week at camp. It could include living in a cabin, eating in the cafeteria, possible activities, and meeting new friends. It is also a good idea to mention the possibility of rain and that sometimes at camp the schedule changes unexpectedly. Social Stories™ will vary because of differences in camp facility, program or routine. Figure 12 gives one example.

Figure 12: Sample Social Story™

Social Narrative for Camp

When I go to camp, I will meet new people and try lots of things. Once I arrive, a counselor will tell us where to park and help us check in. Then I will go to my cabin. Inside, there will be bunk beds and other campers that I will share the cabin with. After I make my bed and get settled, the counselor will tell us more about camp. There are many activities. I might get to ride a horse, swim, paddle a canoe, take a nature hike, shoot a bow and arrow or go on a ropes course. At night, we will have a big event. I might go to a campfire, hayride, scavenger hunt or carnival.

Every day I will get to learn my new schedule. Sometimes at camp it rains and the schedule changes. It is okay to change the schedule because it keeps me safe. When I eat, I will go to the cafeteria with all the other campers. I will see a menu that tells me what my choices for the meal will be. My counselor will show me where to sit and what to do. My counselor is the person I can talk to if I am having a great time, get a little nervous, or if I have a problem. When camp is over, I will be picked up and can go back to my house. Camp is a new adventure.

Parent Information

Similar information may be given to the parents in a different format, outlining what and how best to pack for the child, giving an explanation of the Social Story™ and how to review it with the child, specific information about arrival and drop-off procedures and a reminder to bring any forms and payments not yet turned in. Figure 13 lists items to bring and tips for packing.

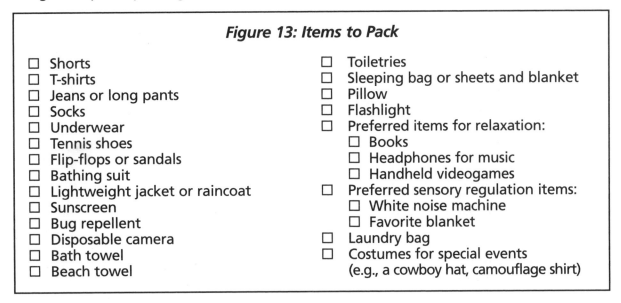

Figure 13: Items to Pack

- ☐ Shorts
- ☐ T-shirts
- ☐ Jeans or long pants
- ☐ Socks
- ☐ Underwear
- ☐ Tennis shoes
- ☐ Flip-flops or sandals
- ☐ Bathing suit
- ☐ Lightweight jacket or raincoat
- ☐ Sunscreen
- ☐ Bug repellent
- ☐ Disposable camera
- ☐ Bath towel
- ☐ Beach towel
- ☐ Toiletries
- ☐ Sleeping bag or sheets and blanket
- ☐ Pillow
- ☐ Flashlight
- ☐ Preferred items for relaxation:
  - ☐ Books
  - ☐ Headphones for music
  - ☐ Handheld videogames
- ☐ Preferred sensory regulation items:
  - ☐ White noise machine
  - ☐ Favorite blanket
- ☐ Laundry bag
- ☐ Costumes for special events (e.g., a cowboy hat, camouflage shirt)

Tips for Packing

In a gallon-size plastic bag, pack one change of clothes containing:
1 pair of shorts
1 t-shirt
1 pair of underwear
1 pair of socks

- Place the bag into a suitcase or trunk, making it easy to pull out one bag and have everything together for the child to wear each day. This alleviates locating one item at a time. Send extra changes of clothing; more than enough for one a day if the child is prone to needing multiple changes.
- Send underwear and socks in abundance to allow for a change of clothes in connection with swimming and other water activities. These items can be packed into separate gallon bags and labeled as "extra socks," etc. Long pants or jeans and a lightweight jacket or rain coat should be included as well, and bags labeled accordingly.
- Label toiletries such as a toothbrush, shampoo, deodorant in a separate bag.
- Make and enclose a list of items that are packed to ensure everything is repacked, especially items brought for relaxation such as videogames or books.
- Label everything!!!
- Send only clothes that are okay to get stained, dirty or torn. Campers will be active and engage in a variety of activities. The first priority of camp is having fun, and taking care of clothes is not generally among the highest priorities.
- Counselors will assist campers in unpacking and organizing their belongings in the cabin to ensure all items are found and used (washing hair with shampoo!).

Miscellaneous Forms

The pre-camp packet also includes several forms pertaining to details of camp. Some camp facilities require permission forms to be signed by parents for the camper to ride a horse or participate on the ropes course, for example. Also, parents may need to sign a form related to insurance coverage while the child is participating in camp activities. Each camp and program will specify which forms are required.

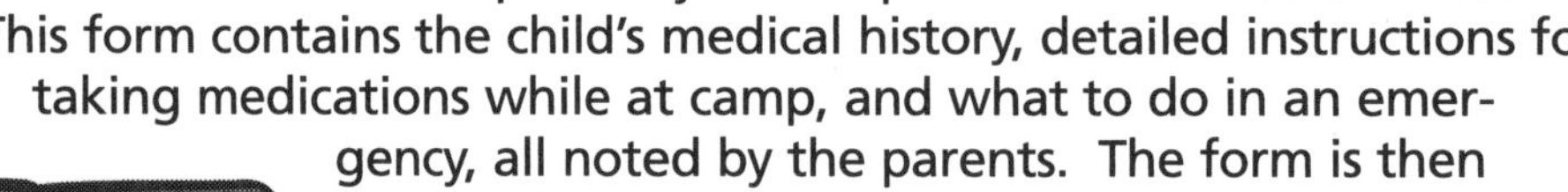

One form that is required by all camp facilities is a health form. This form contains the child's medical history, detailed instructions for taking medications while at camp, and what to do in an emergency, all noted by the parents. The form is then signed and dated and returned to camp. One copy of the completed form is placed in the camper file and another copy in a file to be kept in the medical cabin. Figure 14 displays a list of important information to include on a health form.

Figure 14: Health Form Information

- ✓ Name
- ✓ Age
- ✓ Gender of child
- ✓ Address
- ✓ Two emergency contacts with relationship and phone numbers
- ✓ Medical history
- ✓ Current medical state
- ✓ Medical restrictions
- ✓ Immunizations
- ✓ Allergies
- ✓ Menstrual cycle information
- ✓ Medications brought to camp and procedure for administering them
- ✓ Insurance information
- ✓ Waiver for medical emergency use
- ✓ Parent signature and date

Finalizing the Details

It will come as no surprise that there are many details to planning a successful camp. After the foundational tasks have been taken care of, such as securing a facility, recruiting volunteers, signing up campers and fund-raising, it is time for the leadership team to turn its attention to the details and inner workings of camp to create a minute-to-minute schedule within an atmosphere that supports and encourages campers. By focusing on details, individual components of camp are refined and more fully developed to enhance the experience, safety and success of the camper.

Daily Schedule

Core components of the program consist of daytime and evening activities and other events. Materials should be gathered, staffing needs evaluated and volunteers assigned accordingly. Potential entertainers for evening activities should be screened to find an appropriate program for the campers, and then reserved. Additional volunteers should be recruited to support large evening activities as needed. Figure 15 is an example of a daily schedule.

Figure 15: Daily Schedule	
Time	**Activity**
8:00 am	Breakfast/cabin time
9:00 am	Activity 1: Horseback riding
10:00 am	Activity 2: Group games
11:00 am	Activity 3: Art activity
12:00 noon	Lunch
12:45 pm	Rest time
2:30 pm	Activity 4: Swimming
4:00 pm	Activity 5: Sensory activity
5:30 pm	Cabin time to change into dry clothes
6:00 pm	Dinner
6:45 pm	Evening activity
8:30 pm	Showers/bedtime preparation
10:00 pm	Lights out

As each activity is finalized, the required materials should be noted, as well as ways to enhance the activity with supports or adaptations. For example, a fishing activity requires several types of supplies and supports. Supplies include poles, bait, lures and extra fishing line. To support campers to be successful, make boundaries by placing sticks or a line of rocks for the camper to stand behind on the bank. If the campers fish off a dock, tape may be used to outline spots to ensure each has adequate fishing space. In addition, a visual strip could be created by the leadership team numbering the steps and outlining "how to fish" to be reviewed with the campers before they begin. Figure 16 gives an example of a visual story strip.

Figure 16: Example Story Strip: Instructions for Fishing				
#1 Get a pole and place bait on hook.	#2 Find a spot to stand on the bank or dock.	#3 Toss fishing line into water.	#4 Wait patiently for fish to bite hook.	#5 Pull fish out of water.

T-Shirts

A creative aspect to camp is determining the camp t-shirt. A logo can be developed or the name of camp can be printed in a unique font and displayed centrally on the shirt. T-shirts are distributed to both volunteers and campers. It is recommended that volunteer t-shirts be in a bold color so that they stand out from the campers and are easily spotted both by parents upon arrival at the camp and by the campers throughout the week. Camper t-shirts may be printed on white and tie-dyed as an activity during camp, or printed on a specific color signifying each camper's group. Campers cherish their camp t-shirts as a memento, a keepsake of their week.

Camper Files

Compile a separate folder for each camper to serve as a profile for reference. When a camper's application is received, it should be reviewed by a member of the leadership team and unique details noted on an at-a-glance detail form (see Figure 17) placed in the front of the file, such as parent contact information, need for one-on-one, special diet restrictions, behavioral information, communication system used, and additional appliances the child will bring (e.g., glasses, retainer). This allows important information to be available at a glance to avoid having to search through an entire file for a particular detail later on.

Also develop a list of items and forms that must be turned in by the parents before the camper can participate in camp (see Figure 18). As additional forms are received from the campers, check them off before putting them in the camper's file. In addition to the application, a health form, special activity permission form, where needed, peer references, where applicable, and documentation of payment should be accounted for.

Figure 17: At-A-Glance Detail Form

Child's name ______________________________

Parent contact ______________________________

Address ______________________________

Phone numbers ______________________ ______________________

Check all that apply: Comments:

☐ Needs one-on-one
☐ Special diet
☐ Removable device ☐ glasses ☐ retainer ☐ other: ____________
☐ Additional adaptations ______________________________
☐ Communication system used

Functions

Toileting:	☐ Independent	☐ With some help	☐ Needs full assistance
Eating:	☐ Independent	☐ With some help	☐ Needs full assistance
Bedtime routine:	☐ Independent	☐ With some help	☐ Needs full assistance
Swimming:	☐ Independent	☐ With some help	☐ Needs full assistance
Staying with group:	☐ Independent	☐ With some help	☐ Needs full assistance

Stress triggers:

Motivators:

Other:

Figure 18: Checklist on Front of File

- ☐ Application
- ☐ Health form
- ☐ Special activity permission form (where required)
- ☐ Peer reference letters (where appropriate)
- ☐ Payment in full
- ☐ Payment remaining balance ____________________

Grouping Campers

Once campers have registered and volunteers have been accepted, the matching process can begin. That is, each counselor is given primary responsibility over one to three campers, depending on the ratio of counselors to campers and the number of campers requesting one-on-one support. Cabin members travel and function as a group, but subdividing campers like this allows for a careful watch of each child. Also, if one camper needs to take a break or chooses to not participate in an activity, this arrangement makes it possible for a counselor to sit out with a camper while the others go on with the scheduled activity.

In addition, each counselor should have a list, potentially on the back of his or her nametag, with the daily schedule and indicators of when the camper receives medication. Because many campers will need to visit the medical cabin throughout the day, medication times must be established and posted to ensure a fluid movement. When the counselors gather for training, they will have an opportunity to acquaint themselves with the files for all the campers within their cabin, but with special attention to the campers for whom they are most responsible. If a camper responds exceptionally well to a counselor within the cabin who is not his primary counselor, he may be switched to ensure that all campers are well supported and that the cabin works as a team.

Gathering Materials and Creating Visuals

Making thorough lists of the materials needed at camp and accurately distributing them among activities will contribute to a smooth-running camp. In addition to cabin supplies and items needed for day and evening activities, visuals must be created, sensory items gathered, and games and videos pulled together. Make sure supplies are placed in a central location that is convenient for their intended purpose such as within the cabin or at an event. This way, counselors are not wasting time looking for or fetching items at the last minute for a given activity.

In the following we will take a closer look at supplies and visuals for individual cabins as well as the entire camp.

Visual Supports

Children with ASD respond well to visual instruction, schedules and prompts. Therefore, visual supports are a key support of a successful and smooth-running camp. As illustrated on the following pages, each cabin should have its own set of visual supports in addition to the visuals throughout camp. All visuals are created by the leadership team prior to the start of camp, detailing activities, everyday routines and special events throughout camp. Visuals can be created using Boardmaker™, digital pictures or stick figure drawings. They can be colored or black and white, but should be simple and display the message clearly.

Visuals can also be created for individual campers to assist counselors. Miniature schedules could be printed on the back side of each nametag so that a written form of the schedule is always with each child. In addition, on the counselor's nametag, a list of campers who take medications and the appropriate times should be listed. (*Note:* I do not recommend carrying schedules on bungee cords – the campers do not wear them because they either cause a sensory issue or get in the way at an activity; they can also be a safety issue. Putting the written form of the schedule on the back of the nametag is a more effective way to communicate the information.)

Cabin Visuals

Visuals hung around the cabin serve as reminders, as well as give campers predictability and ease transitions by enabling them to foresee the next activity or the details of a routine. They provide support and a reference on which the camper can rely. Important visuals for the cabin include:

- Choices for cabin time (e.g., rest, read a book)

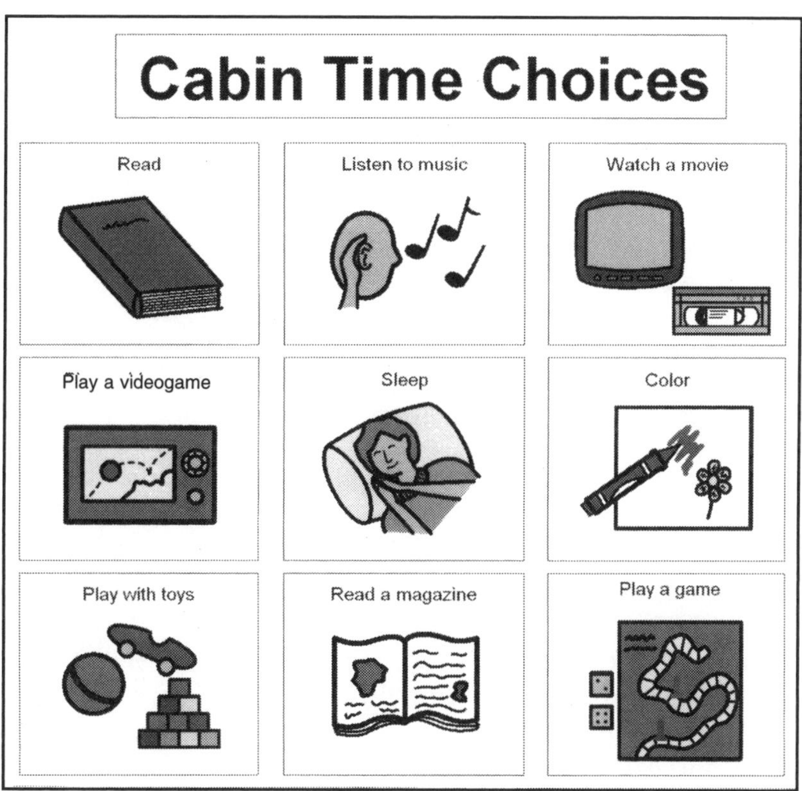

- Morning or evening routines (e.g., how to wash face)
- Countdown strip (e.g., minutes or activities)

Five 5	Four 4	Three 3	Two 2	One 1

- Simple reminders (e.g., put on sunscreen)
- Communication cards or boards (e.g., I need help, wait, quiet)

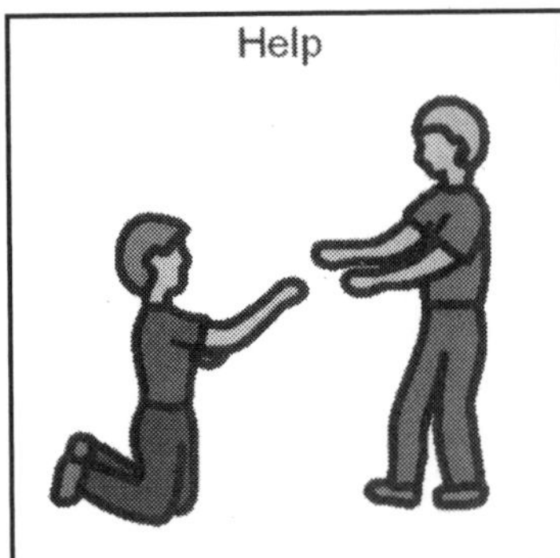

- Work/reward system (e.g., First ___, Then ___; or working for ___)

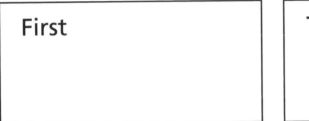

- Menu (e.g., breakfast: bacon, eggs, toast, orange juice)
- Schedule (e.g., breakfast, horses, playground, art, lunch)

In addition, personal miniature schedules can be created for each camper who desires to carry one around. This schedule can be created with the child the night before or in the morning by placing one-inch pictures velcroed down a 6- or 12-inch ruler. As each activity is complete, the camper can remove the icon from his schedule. This gives the camper independence, allows him to foresee the next activity and eases transition.

Campwide Visuals

For general orientation around the camp, post visuals throughout the camp setting. These include items such as posting and maintaining a menu in the cafeteria showing the current and the upcoming meal; signage displaying the theme of the day posted around camp; and prompt strips to assist campers in activities such as how to enter the pool.

In addition, it is often a good idea to post visuals to create boundaries or give parameters to the campers in large-group activities. This would include placing a stick or line of rocks for campers to stand behind on the bank when fishing or creating a boundary in the cafeteria to help show the direction in which the line should move and the distance between children in the line.

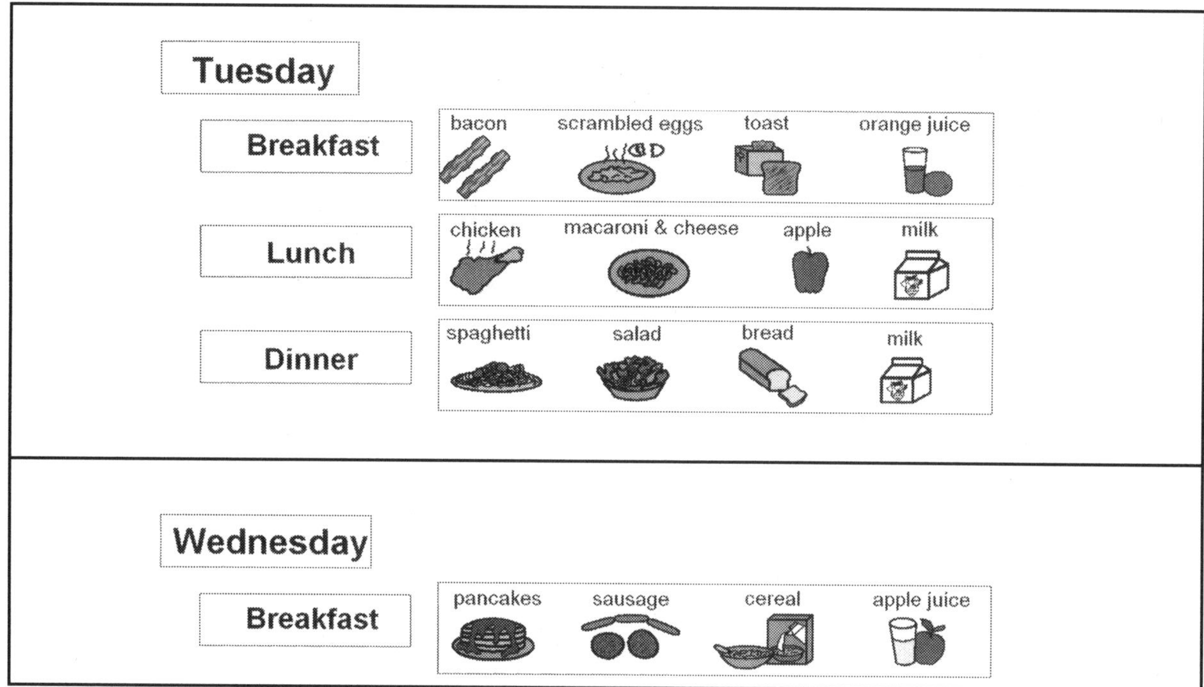

Cabin Supplies

A variety of supplies are needed inside the cabins. Accessible supplies include items from towels to quickly clean up a spill to extra bug repellent for campers who forgot to pack theirs; children may want to make a craft project needing masking tape or markers, or may need a sensory item to fidget or relax. For easiest use, supplies may be divided into separate bins according to their use. For each bin, it helps to tape an inventory sheet to the inside lid of the bin listing all the supplies being distributed. The same list should have a column to inventory remaining supplies so that the bin can be restocked before the next camp begins. Figure 19 gives an example of a supply list.

Figure 19: Sample Cabin Supplies

Cleaning	Sensory	Cabin visuals	Miscellaneous
Ziploc bags Trash bags Window cleaner Cleanser Paper towels Hand towels Sponges	Koosh balls Slinky™ Weighted blanket Flash light Bean bags Foam balls	Mini-schedules How-to strips Relaxation choices Menu Daily schedule	Sunscreen Bug repellent Construction paper Masking tape Markers Glue Scissors Ice breaker games Incident forms Paper sacks First-aid kit Bandages

Campwide Supplies

Numerous supplies are needed for camp in general. Keep them organized in a central location and distributed for each activity or need. Develop a checkout system to keep track of where the supplies are allocated so that they can be shared among the campers throughout their time at camp. Create a page on a clipboard to list the cabin number and the item that is being checked out for the counselors to sign as they take and return items. Place a bin of supplies where they will be used, such as the swimming toys bin by the pool and miscellaneous supplies or the games bin in the cafeteria or medical cabin where campers frequently enter.

Day and Evening Activities

Create a bin for each activity that can remain in its intended activity space, such as a bin for art activities that is not removed for use of art supplies in other areas. Thoroughly list all details of what will be necessary. Even if four activities need similar supplies, equip each activity with its own set of supplies instead of relying on sharing. This ensures that the supplies are plentiful and available when needed. Figure 20 list sample supplies for selected activities.

Figure 20: Sample Activity Bins

Outdoor Equipment	Sensory Fun Materials	Fishing Materials
Football Volleyball Basketball Frisbees Sidewalk chalk Bubbles Checkers	Balloons Buckets Tarps Shaving cream Bubbles Bean bags Fabric tubes Sidewalk chalk	Poles String Bait Story strip: How to fish (see Figure 16) Extra lures and hooks

Snacks

If campers will enjoy an afternoon or evening snack, make a clear plan for distribution of snacks, depending on where they will be consumed. For example, a leadership team member could deliver the snacks to each cabin, a counselor could pick up a bin at lunch and hold it until the appropriate time, or each cabin could visit a snack location and pick up their individual portion. Make sure supplies are carefully planned and clearly labeled, including cups, napkins, number of portions, and so on. Food allergies or special diets must also be taken into account. Finally, alternative snacks brought by individual campers should be available and labeled within the cabin's snack bin.

Games and Videos

A variety of board games, cards, books, videos and music selections should be kept in a central area that can be checked out by a counselor. Such items can be carried around by counselors as alternative options if a camper prefers to not participate in a scheduled activity, or they may be used within the cabin during rest time or cabin free time in the evening.

Counselors must make sure items are returned to the checkout location when they

are no longer being used so that others are able to check them out. If items are few in number, a time limit can be set so that all items will rotate and eventually be available to all campers. If supplies and choices are plentiful, counselors may be encouraged to keep an item as long as it is effective with the campers. Appendix B lists suggestions for a variety of games, books and movies to keep on hand.

Sensory Items

Because most children with ASD have strong sensory needs, it is highly recommended that a variety of sensory items be available. If sensory stimuli are too great such as a loud noise in the cafeteria or lots of movement in a group game, or conversely the stimuli are too low such as a lengthy down time in the cabin because of rain or a nature hike perceived as boring, campers may seek out sensory regulation. Some campers may want to crawl into a tight, dark space that is quiet such as their sleeping bag. Other campers may prefer to run, jump or climb on the bunk beds. Many campers will request to swing at the playground, combining steady, repetitive, predictable movement with less noise or interruption.

Campers should be encouraged to bring their own sensory regulation items from home, such as a favorite blanket or string. However, in case a child did not bring any items, if a bin of sensory items is available, counselors are able to assist campers in regulating their sensory needs. For example, a squishy ball could be picked up on the way to the cafeteria for a restless camper to squeeze while he waits in line. These sensory toys are placed in separate bins from the supplies used in group sensory activities. The items in the supply bins are used in combination with one another with specific instruction, whereas the items in the sensory regulation bins are for immediate use the way they are. Figure 21 lists ideas for what to include in a collection of sensory regulation items.

Figure 21: Sample Sensory Items

- Slinky™
- Soft, squishy balls
- Koosh balls
- Musical instruments
- Bean bags
- Weighted blankets
- Scarf
- Stuffed bean animals
- Flashing light
- Textured blocks
- Fabric tube
- Stretchy bands
- Rain stick

It's a good idea to have multiples of each item available for checkout

Miscellaneous Supplies

It is a good idea to keep a bin of miscellaneous supplies in various areas, such as the medical cabin, cafeteria, and large meeting areas for easy access, in case a camper or counselor leaves something in the cabin or has an emergency need. The items in this bin would be similar to those packed in the cabin miscellaneous bin, such as sunscreen, bug repellent, markers, paper, tape, incident forms and a first-aid kit.

Volunteer and Peer Training

After applications have been reviewed and volunteers selected and notified, it is time to hold staff training. This is an opportunity for the leadership team to reiterate the vision and purpose of camp with the volunteer staff; to equip them with the knowledge and understanding of ASD; and to empower them with tools for a successful experience at camp, such as outlining the schedule, discussing cabin down-time procedures, reviewing protocol for emergency situations, and stressing the importance of attitude and interaction with the campers.

Adult Volunteers

Depending on the distance from which volunteers will have to travel, the leadership team must decide if staff training can occur weeks prior to camp or if it is more efficient to bring volunteers in for training one or two days before camp begins. Build a training agenda that allocates sufficient time to review the purpose and procedures of camp, the daily routine, characteristics of ASD and adaptations that have been made in response to the needs of individual campers, emergency situation protocol, and so on. Make available camper files so the counselors can become familiar with their campers and make note of individual needs and unique characteristics. Plan structured games or relaxed hangout time as opportunities to unify counselors and allow them to acquaint themselves with one another.

If staff training is held several weeks prior to camp, distribute information such as what to bring, health form information, and emergency contact forms and review details about cabins and campers. Campers' files will be available to the counselors for more in-depth review when they arrive at camp to prepare their cabin. If staff training is held only a day or two prior to the start of camp and counselors will remain at the campground, this type of information should be mailed to them ahead of time and brought back to the training. Figure 22 outlines topics to be covered during staff training. Training can last entire days with interaction among volunteers scheduled, or only for a few hours, giving information in a straightforward concise manner. This will depend on when and where staff training is held.

Figure 22: Agenda for Adult Volunteer Training

- ✔ Collect outstanding forms
- ✔ Explain purpose of camp
- ✔ Explain role of each volunteer position
- ✔ Review responsibilities of being a cabin counselor
- ✔ Provide description of campers
- ✔ Review daily camp schedule
- ✔ Review the week in general and special events
- ✔ Arrange for co-counselors to meet and get to know one another
- ✔ Have counselors review camper files and make notes
- ✔ Review emergency protocol
- ✔ Talk through what-if scenarios – brainstorm results as a group
- ✔ Hand out camp t-shirts (to be worn when campers arrive)
- ✔ Answer questions

Peers

In the same manner as the adult volunteers, peer campers should be trained and given expectations for their time at camp. Typically, this meeting is held at the beginning of camp, shortly after all the peers have arrived. At this meeting, peers are first welcomed and given a general overview of camp. Then they participate in a review of activities to help them identify their own strengths and areas of difficulty. This allows them to understand the parallel between themselves and children with ASD.

Characteristics of the campers should be discussed, highlighting that children with ASD have areas of strength, as well as deficits. Empathy and sensitivity to particular aspects and interactions should be discussed as well as ways that the peers can encourage the campers and include them in activities or conversations, defend them if they are being bullied and assist them when activities are difficult or creating frustration. Strategies for communicating and interacting with the campers should be discussed and role-played to simulate cabin scenarios. Figure 23 includes a peer training model.

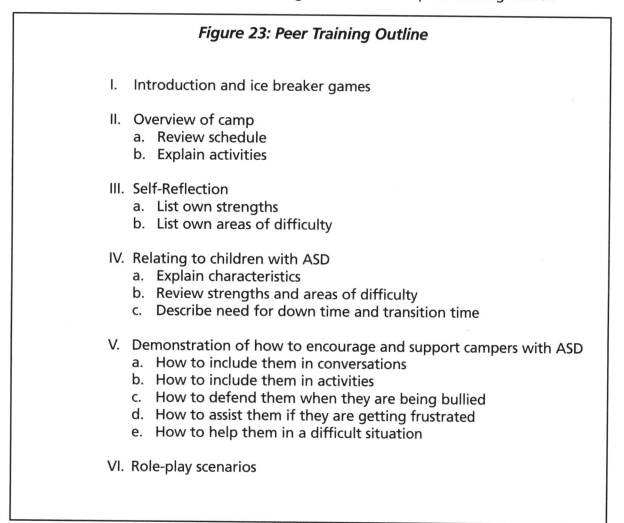

Figure 23: Peer Training Outline

I. Introduction and ice breaker games

II. Overview of camp
  a. Review schedule
  b. Explain activities

III. Self-Reflection
  a. List own strengths
  b. List own areas of difficulty

IV. Relating to children with ASD
  a. Explain characteristics
  b. Review strengths and areas of difficulty
  c. Describe need for down time and transition time

V. Demonstration of how to encourage and support campers with ASD
  a. How to include them in conversations
  b. How to include them in activities
  c. How to defend them when they are being bullied
  d. How to assist them if they are getting frustrated
  e. How to help them in a difficult situation

VI. Role-play scenarios

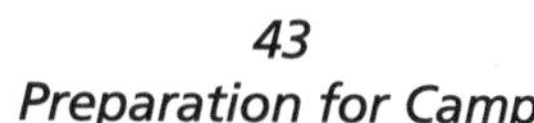

CHAPTER 3
The Camp Experience

Camp is here. All your planning and preparation is about to be put to the test. A camp operates at two levels, the overall management to ensure that all aspects of camp flow fluidly together and the actual goings-on of camp.

Overall Management

The task of overall management belongs to the leadership team, including facilitating the details of each activity, ensuring that the schedule runs smoothly and watching the campers to support and encourage their strengths and challenges. Make sure each counselor fulfills his or her designated role and that communication between the team members is open, including touching base throughout the day about each aspect of camp.

When the counselors arrive a day prior to the campers, all adult volunteers should be gathered to prepare for camp and review necessary protocol. Items to incorporate into this meeting include:

- Allow time for counselors to review camper files for details about their kids (see Chapter 2)
- Answer questions and discuss "what-ifs"
- Distribute supplies and camp t-shirts for all volunteers to wear as the campers arrive and throughout the week
- Distribute walkie-talkies, two per cabin, for communication if the group is separated or to quickly call a member from the leadership team

As a group, all volunteer staff may want to review potential behaviors or circumstances that could occur during camp and the procedure to follow when they do. A plan should be in place for first responders, as well as consequences, paperwork to document the incident, and protocol for allowing those campers not involved to continue with camp. Figure 24 shows an example of an incident report. A completed incident report should be given to the leadership team immediately after it occurs and kept on file as documentation. If a bedwetting incident occurs, discreetly remove the sheets, and wash and replace them with minimal or no attention drawn to the camper. If the incident involves multiple campers or aggressive, frustrated behavior, remove the campers from the situation, separate them and give them quiet down time accompanied by a member of the leadership team. This could take place at the swings, sitting in a cabin or taking a walk. Once the camper has calmed, the behavior or situation is reviewed, detailing what happened, what went well and what could be handled differently next time. Supports can be used to assist this process such as social autopsies, cartooning, the SOCCSS method, creating a Power Card or writing a social narrative (Figure 25 describes these social supports).

Figure 24: Incident Report

- ✔ Name of campers involved
- ✔ Date of incident
- ✔ Time of incident
- ✔ Who observed incident
- ✔ Details of incident
- ✔ Results of incident
- ✔ Signature of campers involved
- ✔ Signature of volunteers

If a consequence is necessary, it should be put into place; however, information and instruction of how to succeed at camp should be taught and be the focus. Behaviors should not be expected to change in one week of camp. Safety for all campers is the top priority. If the camper has repeated behavior instances, the child should be removed from the group or cabin. Several trials of various supports and interventions should be utilized before the camper is dismissed from camp. The goal is to keep all campers at camp for the week and not send anyone home. However, safety must prevail. If a camper repeatedly puts himself or the other campers at risk, this is grounds for dismissal. It is a new environment with new activities and new people. An adjustment with accompanying anxiety should be expected.

During various activities throughout the day George continually makes comments to Javier about how gross and dirty he thinks dogs are. Javier tries to ignore him at first, being the owner and lover of four dogs himself. He tolerates the comments, but becomes increasingly annoyed. Eventually, when George makes a comment about a dog, Javier yells out at him, calling him names and telling him that he wishes George wasn't at camp.

At this point, an incident report should be filled out and the boys debriefed. Otherwise, this easily could be overlooked and not dealt with effectively by, for example, merely separating the boys, asking them to not comment about each other's pets or reminding them that "at camp we use nice words."

In the latter case, because the situation was not fully attended to, later that afternoon in the cabin when George makes another comment about dogs, Javier hops off his bunk and punches George in the mouth. The two boys begin fighting and have to be separated by the counselors. Both boys are overwhelmed, scratched, bleeding and bruised – not just physically, but emotionally as well.

The boys are immediately separated by a distinct distance and any cuts or scrapes are treated. The boys are given time to de-escalate, and then the situation is reviewed. Blame is not assigned, but a review of what occurred and the reactions that took place is conducted. After the boys have cooled down and reviewed the incident, they are brought together and new rules are established for the remainder of camp that will allow them to remain a part of the same group.

Ababio enters the cafeteria with his cabin mates after a long day filled with activities and fun. He is hungry and ready to eat. After filling his plate and getting settled at the table, Ababio does not take a single bite, but begins to fidget in his chair. He covers one ear with his hand and places his elbow on the table, leaning to one side, trying to eat with his other hand. Unsatisfied with this posture, Ababio places both elbows on the table, using both hands to cover both ears and stares down at his food. Still not able to regulate the noise in the cafeteria sufficiently, Ababio finally becomes frustrated and throws his plate of food toward the center of the table.

Tracy, Ababio's counselor, looks surprised at this action. But instead of immediately reprimanding Ababio for his behavior, she looks for clues as to why Ababio threw his plate. Knowing that he is hungry, she asks him if he would like to try another option of food that is being served. Ababio continues to cover his ears and fidget in his chair. Tracy eventually asks Ababio if he would like to take a break from the cafeteria for a few minutes.

When Ababio agrees, Tracy accompanies him outside, where he begins to relax, but complains that he is hungry. Tracy gives Ababio the option to eat outside at the picnic tables where it is quiet and there are fewer people around. Ababio agrees that this would be a good idea. Tracy and Ababio together go back inside to get Ababio a new plate. The other counselors remain at the table with the rest of the cabin, while Ababio and Tracy enjoy a picnic outdoors. Before the next meal, Tracy gives all the campers in her cabin the option to join her outside for a picnic. Some opt to go; however, others enjoy eating indoors where there are no bugs and it is cooler.

Because Tracy was aware of Ababio's tendency to experience sensory overload, she was able to make an adaptation that allowed him to enjoy a

meal successfully. An incident report was still filled out to document the throwing of the plate, the result that no other camper was hit by it, and that the incident prompted the removal from the cafeteria for Ababio's benefit. The solution (eating outside) was not used as a punishment, but offered as an alternative open to all campers within the cabin.

Figure 25: Social Supports

Social Autopsy (Lavoie, cited in Bieber, 1994)

Assists campers in reviewing social mistakes and is designed to decrease the likelihood that the same social error will be repeated. The camper is asked to review the encounter, identify the error, identify those affected by the error, figure how to correct the error and create a plan so that the error does not occur again.

Cartooning

Uses simple drawings and conversation bubbles to illustrate and diagram a social encounter in a comic strip-like format. The camper is able to diagram a situation into steps, detailing and narrating each piece of the process.

SOCCSS (Jan Roosa, 1995; cited in Myles & Southwick, 2005)

Allows camper to put social interaction into a sequential form, describing what happened within a situation. It encourages problem solving, using cause and effect to demonstrate the camper's own influence over a situation.

Power Card (Gagnon, 2001)

Utilizes a camper's special interest to create a story and three to five detailed reminders for the camper to rely on when encountering a social situation.

Social Narrative

Written from the camper perspective by an adult volunteer, it describes social cues and appropriate responses that could be demonstrated in a social setting. It is used to prepare/prime campers to encounter a new setting or interaction and to teach social skills. It encourages self-awareness and gives a broader perspective to the situation.

After the group meeting, counselors are dismissed to set up their cabins, post visuals, create a welcoming atmosphere and put away their own personal items so that when the campers arrive, their full attention can shift to their support and welfare.

During this time, the leadership team continues to set up the details of camp, such as allocating supplies and labeling cabins and parking areas, so that once camp begins, families can flow with ease through the registration and drop-off procedure and activities can get off to a good start.

Opening of Camp

Greeting and Arrival

How smoothly the arrival of the campers and their transition to camp goes will set the tone for the week. Greet campers with enthusiasm and connect them to their cabin mates as soon as possible so that they can begin to get acquainted, perhaps by working together on a project that's already set up. They need to feel welcomed and comfortable in their new surroundings from the very beginning.

When a car arrives at the entrance of camp, the family should be greeted by a member of the camp staff. This gesture not only ensures the family that they have arrived at the right place, it is a nice welcome and a convenient way to give directions for where to park and check in. If the number of staff allows, it is recommended that a person be paired with a family as they arrive. One or two counselors from each cabin should participate in the initial greeting process, while the other counselors remain in the cabin to receive the campers as they enter.

As the family parks in the main parking lot, the counselor helps them unload and ushers them to the registration check-in table. Some camp facilities have staff members who will then transport the campers' luggage to the appropriate cabin for them while the family checks in. The counselor introduces herself to the child and fills out nametags for each member of the family. Once the child is connected to somebody at the registration table, the counselor can return to the entrance to greet another family. If the camp facility allows the family to drive all the way to the cabin to unload, leave all the camper's items in the car while going through the registration process. The family should still be stopped, greeted and registered as they enter camp before going straight to the cabin.

Registration Table

At the registration table, a list of what to discuss with the parents when they check in is helpful as a reference to ensure that nothing is forgotten or left out during what is often a hectic procedure. Figure 26 presents a checklist of steps in the registration process.

A system consisting of a file for each child in alphabetical order will help make the check-in process run smoothly. Files should be flagged if anything still needs to be turned in before the camper can participate in camp (see Chapter 2). The file should include information that is specific for the camper, such as a nametag with a schedule printed on the back, the camper's cabin assignment, and group name or color.

Make sure to have plenty of extra forms and pens at the registration table so that parents who forgot a form are able to fill it out when they check in. Depending on the layout of camp, it is often helpful to have maps to hand out so families can easily find their way to the child's cabin, to the medical cabin to drop off medications, and to the cafeteria if they have special food items to deliver.

Volunteers at the registration table checking in campers should be adequate in number for the volume of campers expected (1 volunteer to every 10 campers). This allows parents to quickly get their camper checked in and transitioned to the cabin. The first experience of camp should not be waiting in a line. A couple of members from the leadership team should be "roamers" in the registration area, free to jump in where needed if there are questions or an unexpected incident.

Figure 26: Checklist of Steps in the Registration Process

- ☐ Check that all forms are on file
- ☐ Give out nametags to camper and family members
- ☐ Hand out cabin assignment
- ☐ Distribute map of campground
- ☐ Hand out parent packet:
  - Counselor biography
  - Highlights of the week
- ☐ Review the following steps with parents:
  - Check in at cabin
  - Check in with medical cabin and drop off medications
  - Drop off food in cafeteria

Finding and Settling in the Cabin

After the family has completed the final registration/check-in steps, they can walk (or drive) the child and his belongings to the assigned cabin where the child is greeted by his counselor and introduced to other campers for the week. Depending on the set-up of the camp, the parents may be allowed to stay and help the child unpack his things, but the counselor should take the initiative for making each child feel comfortable. For example, be ready to offer assistance when beds are being made. It is a good idea to make the bed soon after the child arrives at the cabin so that he feels he has his own space. Once the bedding is on, the child can open his belongings and get settled.

The counselor should visit with the parent to double-check that the registration protocol has been completed, including visiting the medical cabin and cafeteria if necessary. Also find out if a camera was packed and make a note of it so that pictures can be taken throughout the week. In addition, the counselor should review with the parents what special items were brought for relaxation time and if the child has any particular routines of which the cabin should be aware. It is always nice to ask the parents if there is "anything else" they would like to share about their child even if such information has already been collected via various forms as part of the registration process.

The counselors should help the campers unpack, locating items such as toothbrush, shampoo, bathing suit and tennis shoes, and assisting with organization so that items are easy to locate and use throughout the week. After the camper has unpacked, help him begin an activity such as playing with other campers or making a name sign for his bed to personalize his space to make the transition of settling in and parents leaving easier.

It is a good idea to hold a meeting for just parents at a certain time so that parents do not linger too long. At such a meeting, give a brief overview of the week to assure parents that their children are in for a wonderful experience; also review pick-up procedures. If no parent meeting is held, it is nice to give the parents a packet of information containing a brief biography of their child's counselors, an overall review of the week and highlights of evening events. This can be distributed by the counselors in the cabin or given out at the registration table when the family arrives.

Once all of the campers have arrived in the cabin, the beds have been made, all items have been unpacked and arranged, and all parents have left, counselors meet with the campers to welcome them to camp and introduce them to one another. Ice breaker games can be played to get the campers acquainted. After the campers are somewhat familiar with their cabin mates, allow them as a group to determine the rules for their time at camp. Having the campers list what is important to them and establish the boundaries gives them ownership and encourages their participation in following the rules.

Counselors can shape the brainstorm session by asking questions about a particular aspect of camp such as "What rules should we make about the bathroom?" As rules and guidelines are verbalized, a counselor should write them down so that they can be posted. When the campers have created all the rules they can think of, counselors can add items that will encourage safety, rest, and an overall successful week for the campers. Campers can then discuss the importance of the rules.

Dana, the counselor, facilitated the rule-creating session with her cabin. She asked the campers to think of all the rules that should be a part of camp. Amber volunteered that it was important to her to have her clothes by her bed so they did not get lost. Suzy said that it would be nice to turn the lights off when they were done in the bathroom. Jessica said that at camp only nice words should be used.

Dana agreed that all of these were great rules and wrote them down on a poster to be hung in the cabin. She then asked, "What would be an important rule about leaving the cabin?" The girls thought for a moment. Suzy said that she thought everyone should leave together. Dana responded that sometimes only one or two campers need to leave the cabin such as when they go to get their medicines, but that a good rule would be to only leave the cabin if a counselor was with them. All the girls agreed that this would be a smart choice and a good rule.

Programming

Programming is at the heart of camp. Children with ASD need structure and routine and thrive on predictability. However, good programming does not necessarily mean a schedule packed full of activities. Transition time must be carefully planned for, as well as meals and rest times.

Giving the campers guidelines and a schedule allows them to anticipate the changes that occur throughout the day by setting expectations while giving them flexibility within the established boundaries. In other words, the children can predict the length of an activity as well as look forward to a preferred activity that still awaits them.

Wake-Up and Breakfast Routine

Starting when the child awakes, a plan must be in place for every moment of the day. Is the child allowed to get out of bed to find an activity to do quietly while the rest are still asleep or must he remain in bed until the alarm sounds, signaling that it is alright to move around? Because children wake up at different speeds, the morning routine should be reviewed the night before. The child can help by choosing the clothes he would like to wear the next day and setting them out on the top of his trunk or suitcase. Together, review the child's typical morning routine at home and how it is the same or different from the morning routine in the cabin. For example, at camp the child may want to wash his face and use the restroom before changing out of his pajamas. Once the child is ready, a waiting activity such as watching a video, playing a game with another camper, or quietly reading should be in place so that the child remains occupied until all of the children in the cabin are ready for breakfast.

Once all the campers in the cabin are ready, the group travels to breakfast together. If unplanned, mealtimes can be a trap for unoccupied time where the campers fidget, become restless or even begin to pick on one another. Depending on how meals are served, campers may need to be staggered in the dining hall in order to avoid having to wait in a long line. The camp may choose to serve family style once all the campers have arrived and are seated at their respective tables. Counselors should be familiar with the serving style and plan accordingly when moving the campers to the dining hall so the children are not waiting unnecessarily. If space allows, a large jigsaw puzzle can be placed on a table for campers to work on once they have finished their meal. Some campers may prefer to bring an individual activity to do at their seat such as reading a book. Having an established routine and an activity makes the wait time and transition go more smoothly.

Daily Activities

Once breakfast is over, the morning activities begin. A typical day contains five to six activities, three to four in the morning and two to three in the afternoon. Depending on the activity and the preset campsite schedule, the length and number of activities vary. The average length of an activity, such as social skills group, should be about 45 minutes, allowing for transition time prior to and in between each activity for clean-up and travel time, totaling one hour on the schedule. Some activities, such as swimming, require more time and span for one hour and a half.

Again, allow time prior to and after the activity for transition, for campers to wind down, to gather any materials that were brought with them, to look at their schedules to determine where to go for the next activity, to actually travel to the next place and finally to prepare to begin the activity.

Campers transition from one activity straight to the next, allowing them to continuously be engaged versus creating a lot of unnecessary wait time or down time between activities. If several cabins are gathering to participate in the same activity together, immediately engaging the campers will assist in maintaining their attention and participation while waiting for everyone to arrive. Beginning the activity without all the campers is not always feasible because specific instructions may need to be given for safety such as in archery, so a quick ice breaker game could be played to fill in the time until all the campers arrive.

Types of Daytime Activities

When planning the schedule, take into account the type of activity, travel time across the campground from one activity to the next, as well as the intensity of participation.

Some activities require more involvement, physically or intellectually, and if scheduled next to one another, will wear out the campers faster than if they are spread out with less taxing activities in between. Intermix activities that can be completed as an individual or activities that are calming with activities that require group participation or lots of motion. Balancing the schedule with these considerations in mind encourages camper participation and sustains involvement.

Further, activities that require materials to be brought along or certain attire be worn should be grouped together to reduce transition time back to the cabin between activities. It also makes for a more pleasant experience if campers are not lugging around unnecessary materials or if wet, messy clothes are not worn for an extended period of time. These considerations are particularly important for children with ASD, many of whom have sensory issues. No one enjoys riding a horse in a wet bathing suit!

The following are typical activities that would be a part of most camp experiences. They may need to be adapted for children with ASD to ensure these campers are supported for success, but there are few camp activities that should be discouraged altogether. This will depend on the particular group of campers attending, their strengths, needs and abilities. Activities should be offered to those willing and able to participate. However, if a camper chooses to not attempt an activity, that's alright. After all, it is summer camp.

Social Group

Reviewing appropriate social skills and building self-esteem with campers gives them an opportunity to interact in a safe and friendly environment. Social interactions are a challenge for many children with ASD, who need to be coached on topics such as introductions, conversation skills, entering and exiting a group, and perspective taking. This type of activity gives a structured time to talk about camp or a topic of the day and allows for skills to be demonstrated and practiced. Use of role-plays and scenarios helps to enhance the camp experience. Appendix A lists social skill and self-esteem building activities. In addition, Appendix C lists several resources to assist in constructing the purpose, framework and structure of the group.

Games that reinforce these topics can be played to put skills into practice. For example, campers could pair up and interview one another and then return to the group and introduce each other. This activity could be enriched by having each child create a poster using words or pictures to describe his partner.

Horseback Riding

Horseback riding is a fun activity for most children at camp because it is something they usually do not get to do at home. In addition to the sheer joy of a new experience, during horseback riding children learn life skills by having to follow a sequenced procedure in preparing for and actually riding the horse. Besides, they demonstrate balance and independence all the while riding along a trail in line with their peers. An adult should walk next to each rider. The camp will most likely have pre-established regulations and staff that assist with this activity.

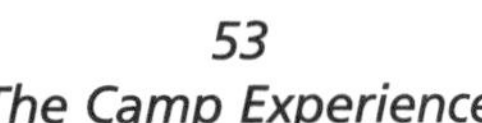

Group Games

These types of games are wonderful for bringing the group together. They encourage interaction and expression as well as physical activity and teamwork. Games such as team relays, elbow tag, *Red Rover, Duck Duck Goose, I Never, Red Light Green Light* or *Simon Says* are favorites among campers. More sedentary group games include *"telephone," charades, Pictionary,* and *Hangman.*

Fishing

Nothing starts the day out like a fishing trip. Campers have the opportunity to assist in baiting their hook and, if lucky, enjoy the thrill of catching a fish. Poles can be made from long sticks by tying a string to one end. The campers can search the ground for a stick to make their own pole or can use one already made. While they wait, it is a good time to talk about establishing personal space, staying quiet and being patient – all challenges for children with ASD. Campers can rotate between spots along the edge of the water or on the dock to find the place where the fish are biting. Each camper must sustain focused attention as they watch for a bite or a tug on the line. However, once a fish is caught, campers can work together to bring in their catch. Campers must be carefully assisted by an adult when baiting or removing a fish from a hook.

Archery

New to most children, this activity requires instruction and careful supervision. It teaches the campers aim, technique and detail. Depending on the campsite, campers may shoot in groups of three or four. Because of the length of time it takes to set up, shoot, and retrieve arrows, campers may have multiple turns or only one round. These details are important to communicate in advance so that the children will know what to expect and understand when the activity is finished.

Playground Time

This time can be used for relaxing free play. A variety of balls and toys should be left out to pick up and play with at leisure, such as frisbees, basketballs, jump ropes, horseshoes, or a volleyball. It is a good idea to locate this activity near a swing set or playground to add other choices. Some children prefer to sit and swing whereas others will be ready to gather a group and play basketball.

This is a nice opportunity to allow the campers to choose for themselves how they would like to spend their time. As always, however, they must be supervised. Some campers may choose to use this time to rest and not engage in an activity at all. A nearby spot in the shade can be the resting place for campers. At least one counselor should stay with the resting campers.

Ropes Course

When available, ropes courses are typically reserved for the oldest campers. This can be a special time, challenging children to move beyond their limits and push themselves to try new things. The activity builds camaraderie because campers must work together, cheer for one another, and trust that their task can be accomplished. Specific instruction accompanied by visuals will assist in the explanation of new activities and tasks. This activity can vary in time from one activity period through the whole morning, depending on the facilities available.

Some camp facilities have high-ropes (challenge) courses. These typically consist of a series of individual obstacles strung through the treetops. It can be overwhelming and very challenging for some children. Campers may want to do this with a counselor or in tandem if possible. As an alternative, many camp facilities have low elements, consisting of group building activities that are low to or even on the ground. These activities may be a better choice. They allow the campers to work together and support one another and do not create as many balance or height difficulties for the campers.

Regardless of level of difficulty, these activities require a lot of guidance as well as support and encouragement. Activities such as the pamper pole or flying swing, which are sometimes part of a high-ropes course, should be avoided in most cases.

Rhythm and Movement

Rhythm and movement offers fun opportunities for campers to use their imaginations, pay attention to their bodies and shake things up a little. Play an assortment of musical genres in the background, giving variation to rhythm and beat. Offering scarves, hats, jackets, sunglasses, and dress-up items that are appealing to both girls and boys enhances their expression and expands their imagination. Using a larger number of participants and an extensive range of items typically elicits a higher rate of participation. Songs that are typically accompanied by specific motions such as the chicken dance or YMCA could be played to get the group moving. Other music selections include a mixture of classical, hip-hop, country, nature sounds and rhythmic beats, varying the speed and types of movements elicited by campers.

Hiking/Nature Walk

Most of the campers enjoy a nature walk to explore the grounds around them. To enhance the journey, encourage them to bring along a small bag to collect interesting items or have them rotate as the leader, making up adventures and discovering new areas. Have the campers mark the path so that they can find their way back. Establish a time limit to set a parameter for turning around and heading back towards the entrance. This activity can be used as a time-filler if another activity has finished early. Most campers enjoy exploring even for a few minutes.

Art Activity

During art, it is a good idea to offer several choices to keep the campers engaged for the entire time scheduled. Fun camp art ideas include tie-dying t-shirts, socks or bandannas, making bead necklaces or decorating address books. Campers can also create a journal, adding a colored picture each day of a favorite activity or memory of camp. Appendix A lists several art activities that could be used in the camp setting.

Rest Time

After the morning activities, campers eagerly desire lunch and are ready for rest. Rest time is just as important as an active activity and should be scheduled like any other part of the program. During rest time, the campers are encouraged to be alone, perhaps on their individual beds. Napping is recommended, but quiet activities such as reading, playing a videogame or coloring are appropriate choices. As the campers play quietly alone,

often they fall asleep out of exhaustion from the morning's activities and the fresh air. Depending on the length of the rest time scheduled, if campers would like to gather in pairs to play a quiet game inside the cabin, it is recommended that this be offered as an option during only the second half of rest time, allowing those who would like to rest and who need sleep to do so.

Swimming

Most children love to swim at summer camp. Whether diving off the diving board or throwing balls around in the shallow end, swimming is a highlight for most campers. When planning and executing this activity, it is important to consider each child's swimming level and ability. A swim test is recommended on the first day to observe those who can swim without assistance in the deep end. Levels of ability can be indicated by having children wear special bracelets or other markings. Keep children who are unable to swim in the shallow water and monitor them carefully. This activity allows the children to relax and enjoy socializing while still being physically active as they move around the pool.

Canoeing

Canoeing can be fun, but it is a labor-intensive activity. Since typically many children have not participated in canoeing prior to the camp experience, it is recommended that one counselor be in each canoe of two or three children. Further, a short venture is recommended, and life jackets must be worn at all times. The campers will enjoy paddling around in a small area, singing camp songs or talking about camp. For the more adventuresome and capable, two canoes can race one another back to the beach or can hold on to one another while sitting out in the water. It is an enjoyable group activity.

Sensory Activities

These activities should be scheduled with other wet or messy activities and, most preferably, before a cabin break or a dive into the pool. During sensory time, a variety of activities can be set out, allowing the campers to move back and forth. Activities include shaving cream baths, rolling around on a tarp or throwing clumps of shaving cream onto one another. A water balloon toss is another fun and refreshing activity, as is blowing giant bubbles with a variety of blowers. Children can also participate in an obstacle course or team relays. Fabric tubes, bean bags, punching bags or sidewalk chalk also give the campers a sensory outlet if they prefer not to participate in the wet or messy items. Appendix A lists several sensory activities.

Evening Activities

Evening activities are a wonderful time to create special group memories with the campers. Entertainers can be brought in or themes can be established to create an atmosphere that the campers will not soon forget. Give campers a list of evening activities and events prior to arriving at camp so that they can pack a costume or item that can be used as part of the activity.

While the event is taking place, give campers the option to take a break and remove themselves if needed. Large groups or lots of motion or noise can be disruptive to some campers. After the child has had an opportunity to calm down and readjust, immediately reintroduce him to the activity, giving him the choice to participate with adaptations if needed. Below are a few suggestions for favorite evening activities.

Juggler/Magician

Children are fascinated by jugglers and magicians. When choosing this type of performer, review his or her work ahead of time to make sure it is suitable for the campers; that is, age- and content-appropriate. With proper preparation, encourage the performer to incorporate volunteers into his act to engage the children instead of having them merely observe.

Olympics

This activity encourages group participation and can be as small or as large an event as the staff and campers make it. Team names, mottos and cheers can be generated. Signs can be made and carried to each event. Bandannas or a specifically colored shirt can be worn to signify unity of the team. A variety of activities such as relay races can be run and can include both individual and team events.

Open Swim Party

Because swimming is such a preferred activity at camp, one evening can be dedicated to open swim. Special events can be held such as crazy jumps or cannon ball contests from the diving board. Provide tool toys and arrange group games.

Theme Party

Theme parties are a huge hit at camp because the campers have the opportunity to dress up or assume different roles. Have children wear costumes or simply hang signs around campers' necks to indicate their role. If music and snacks are a part of the party, make sure they fit the theme as well. Popular themes include the following:

Mission Impossible: Campers dress up in camouflage and go on a campwide scavenger hunt; the theme song for *Mission Impossible* could be played to fire up campers and send them off on their journey.

Pirates: Campers dress up as pirates, wearing stripes and an eye patch. To add to the excitement the adult volunteers can perform a skit dressed up as pirates, claiming that there is a treasure at camp. Each cabin receives a map leading them around camp to their own treasure. A piñata could be the treasure found at the end with small prizes inside instead of candy. Campers can return to a large meeting area after they find their treasures and watch the movie *Peter Pan.*

Western Night: Dress in denim, hats, boots or bandannas and have a hayride, campfire with s'mores, followed by a square dance with a variety of upbeat country songs.

Carnival

Set up multiple activities at one time for the campers to move through in small groups. Award prizes for attempting the various activities to encourage campers to repeat each activity several times. Larger prizes can be awarded for particular feats to keep the campers interested in achieving a goal. Carnival booths might include activities such as a dunking booth, jump house, sock toss, ring toss, fishing for a prize, dart throwing, cookie decorating, cotton candy or ball toss. The atmosphere can be enhanced with music, balloons, and clowns or special guests roaming the field.

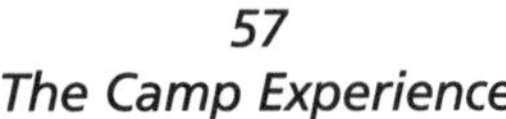

Game Night

Game night provides an atmosphere that invites the campers to come together and challenge one another in their favorite games. Games such as checkers, chess, *UNO*, theme trading card games, *Connect Four* or *Guess Who* are quick turn-over games that campers can engage in repeatedly.

Ping-pong, foose ball or air hockey tables may also be set up, preferably in a large room with space both for the players and for spectators waiting their turn. Depending on the campers, tournaments could be arranged to build excitement, or games could just be played without the additional competitiveness.

Movie Night

Movie night can be arranged as an all-camp activity or individually for each cabin if adequate equipment is available. Choose a gender-neutral, age-appropriate film. Serve popcorn and drinks (or suitable alternatives) and encourage campers to wear their pajamas or bring their pillows to the event. This is a relaxing way to end the evening.

CHAPTER 4

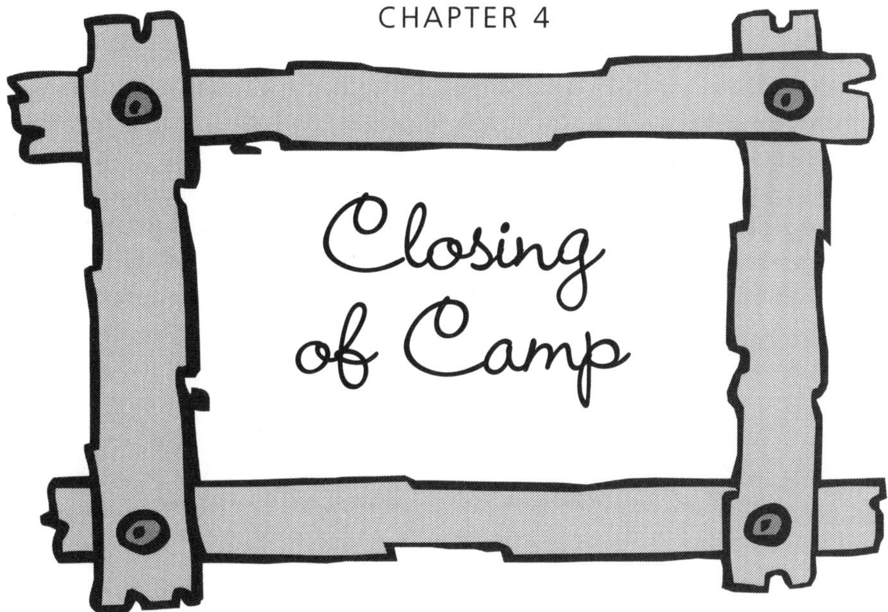

Closing of Camp

After the camp experience with its unforgettable moments and sometimes life-altering events, a somewhat mundane task remains: close of camp. Preparing the campers for the close of camp is a process. All items – whether camp supplies or children's personal belongings – must be gathered and repacked, and cabins cleaned. As campers find their items and tuck them away, move the bags out onto the porch, sidewalk or the front room to clear space in the cabin. Place unclaimed items in a lost-and-found area for review and identification by the parents. Campers leave with more than they arrived with because they may have put their dirty laundry into a separate bag throughout the week or have accrued new items from nature hikes and art projects. Each camper should have a clearly labeled space with his name where his bags and items are placed to be picked up by the parents. Any remaining medications or food items should also be retrieved and placed with the campers' things.

Once the cabin begins to clear out and become less crowded, cleaning can begin. Typically, the camp facility requires that a series of cleaning jobs be completed before the cabin can be checked out. Involve campers by having them gather trash, rinse sinks or showers, sweep the floor and return items to their appropriate bins to be inventoried.

Camp has come to a close, and it is time to conclude and dismiss the campers back to their parents. The nature of the camp site will somewhat dictate how the closing procedures occur. For example, whether parents will be able to drive back to the cabins in order to pick up campers' belongings or if all items, labeled for each camper, have to be carried to a central point by a main parking area.

As the culmination of the camp experience, a large meeting is encouraged to gather all parents and campers. A slide show or video from the week can be shown and counselors can share highlights. Campers may want to put on a skit or sing a song that they have worked on all week. This gives the parents an opportunity to see their children interacting with others.

It is also encouraged that counselors hand out awards or character quality certificates to each camper (Figure 27 shows an example certificate). This festive ceremony can take place in front of the entire group or in a smaller gathering of just the cabin members and their families. (If campers must return to their cabins to retrieve their belongings, this provides an opportunity to gather and hand out these items.) The purpose of this activity is to build upon and celebrate the child's strengths. If a humorous incident or special encounter occurred, an award could be given out as a reminder; however, in general, awards should not be sarcastic. In addition, if pictures were taken throughout the week, one or two photographs of each child could be printed and distributed to the parents to give them an immediate look at how their child participated throughout the week.

Figure 27: Character Quality Certificate

James Crawford
At Camp River Bend
June 14-17, 2005
Demonstrated these character qualities

loyalty

dependability

(Add your personal note here)

Signed by counselors	*Signed by counselors*

Final Wrap-Up

Once all campers have been dismissed to their parents, counselors gather up their cabin supplies and bring them to a central meeting point. Then all the volunteers gather to review the week and debrief. Stories can be shared and moments remembered. Ask each volunteer to complete an evaluation to highlight what went well and to make suggestions for what could help camp run better the next time. Figure 28 shows an example evaluation form.

In addition, it is a nice touch to have all the counselors write a brief note to each family, sharing a highlight of the child's week. Parents love to hear what is special about their child and how he or she is growing and participating in activities. Having the counselors write letters at the close of camp ensures that they get done and that each camper is still fresh on the counselor's mind. A sample postcard outlining what to include makes the

volunteer's task easier. Figure 29 shows a simple note for parents that can be replicated. Collect the notes and mail them within the following week to follow up with the families and campers. A group camp picture could be included as well.

Figure 28: Volunteer Evaluation Form

Please circle appropriate number and leave a comment for each item.

	Excellent 4	Good 3	Fair 2	Poor 1	Comments
Pre-camp activities					
Recruitment process	4	3	2	1	
Information received prior to arrival	4	3	2	1	
Orientation	4	3	2	1	
Camp					
Arrival process	4	3	2	1	
List daily activities separately:					
Art	4	3	2	1	
Horses	4	3	2	1	
Nature hike	4	3	2	1	
List evening activities separately:					
Carnival	4	3	2	1	
Olympics	4	3	2	1	
Hayride	4	3	2	1	
Square dance	4	3	2	1	
Departure process	4	3	2	1	
Food	4	3	2	1	
Cabins	4	3	2	1	
Overall camp experience	4	3	2	1	

Anything else:

Figure 29: Example Letter to Parents

Dear Mr. and Mrs. Smith,

It was wonderful to meet your son *(child's name)* this week at camp. I was one of his counselors and was able to observe him throughout the day.

Give specific examples ... He always seemed to enjoy swimming at the pool, and catching a fish was the highlight of his week. In the cabin he enjoyed playing cards with the other boys and was always willing to try a new activity.

Camp was a success for *(child's name)* and I hope he will have opportunity to go again next year. I am glad I was able to hang out with him this week.

Sincerely,
Counselor's name

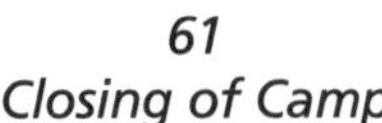

Once the volunteers have turned in all their items and bins, written their letters and completed their evaluations, they are dismissed. Although camp is technically over, there will be lingering details for members of the leadership team to take care of in the following days and weeks. This includes paying outstanding bills, reviewing evaluations, and writing up adaptations for future camps with implications for the budget, schedule, and overall camp protocol.

Other wrap-up activities include sending notes to volunteers, both individuals and groups from the community, thanking them for their participation and highlighting a strength they displayed or a story that occurred. A group camp picture is another welcome remembrance along with information about future events to elicit continued participation.

When "everything" is done, the leadership team may want to celebrate or individually reflect on the various aspects of camp, understanding that it will continue to change and grow over time. Take a deep breath and know you have done well!

Appendix

Appendix A

Group Activities

ICE BREAKERS

Toilet Paper Squares
Have campers sit in a circle. Pass a roll of toilet paper around the circle, asking the campers to take the number of squares they would like. After the roll has gone all the way around, have each camper tell one thing about themselves for each square that they are holding.

Bingo
Create a 5"x5" grid that contains an interesting personal fact about individual campers in each square such as "Has been to Kentucky." Make a copy for each camper and distribute. Have the children ask one another questions about the facts on the paper. If they find someone who matches the item in the square, that camper signs the spot. The campers continue to ask one another questions until they have filled their card.

Ball Toss Name Game
Campers gather in a circle. One ball is introduced at the beginning to be tossed around the circle. As the ball is tossed, the camper throwing the ball says the name of the camper it is going to. This continues around the circle. If the campers are up for the challenge, a second or third ball could be introduced, keeping all balls going at the same time.

"All My Neighbors"
Campers sit in chairs in a circle. One person stands in the middle and says "All my neighbors who have ____" and fills in the blank (e.g., white shorts). Anyone who has the mentioned item must stand and change chairs with another camper. In the end, one person will be without a chair and is the next person to call the phrase.

I've Never ...
Campers sit in chairs in a circle. One person is in the middle and says "I've never _____" and fills in the blank (e.g., seen an elephant). Anyone who has done the mentioned item must stand and change chairs with another camper. In the end, one person will be without a chair and is the next person to call the phrase.

Two Truths, One Lie
Campers write down three statements about themselves on an index card, two that are accurate and one that is made up. Once all the campers have finished writing their statements (could be dictated to a counselor), each goes around the circle and reads all three items that they wrote (again, a counselor or peer camper can help if the camper has trouble reading). The other campers have to determine which one is the made-up statement.

ART ACTIVITIES

Tie-Dye T-Shirts
Materials:

- Bucket – one per color
- Dye
- Water
- Clothes pins
- Rubber bands
- Clothes line

What you do:
Dissolve each color dye in warm water in a separate bucket. Gather small portions of the t-shirt and wrap them in rubber bands. Repeat several times all over the shirt. Dip the rubber-banded portions into the various dyes or submerge the whole shirt in one color until the shirt absorbs the color. Clothes-pin the still rubber-banded shirt to the line to dry. After the shirt has completely dried, remove the rubber bands to see the design.

Journal
Materials:

- Large sheet of construction paper
- White copy paper
- Stapler
- Markers or crayons

What you do:
Fold a large piece of construction paper in half, making the cover of the journal. Place 8 to 10 sheets of white paper inside the colored construction paper and staple to make a book. Have the child decorate the cover of the journal and draw a picture or write a story each day reflecting a part of camp. Counselors and activity coordinators can write down the narrations to the pictures if needed.

Picture Frame
Materials:

- Popsicle sticks
- Precut paper
- Foam shapes
- Markers
- Glue

What you do:
Connect the popsicle sticks together with glue, making a square or rectangle shape and decorate with markers or foam shapes. Have the campers draw a picture of their friends at camp on a precut paper to fit the shape of the frame. Glue the picture to the back side of the frame so that the picture is framed by the decorated side.

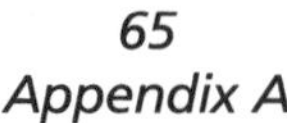

Pillow Cases
Materials:
- Pillow case
- Permanent marker
- Cardboard

What you do:
Give each camper a solid-colored pillow case, preferably white. Place a piece of cardboard inside the pillow case to prevent the markers from bleeding through. Have campers write their name in large letters in the center and decorate their pillow case with pictures that describe them or camp. Other campers can sign the pillow cases, creating a memory of camp.

Friendship Bracelet
Materials:
- Embroidery thread
- Variety of beads
- Safety pins

What you do:
Teach the campers a variety of ways to knot their thread to create a bracelets, such as braiding, four-strand single knots or fishtailing. The campers could also simply string a variety of beads onto the embroidery thread to create patterns or their names. Tie all the strands of thread together in a knot at the top. To allow the child to take the unfinished bracelet with him or to hold the thread more steady, place a safety pin through the knot and attach to a pillow, shirt or pant leg.

Chalk Salt
Materials:
- Baby food jars or small clear jars
- Colored sidewalk chalk
- Salt
- Bowls – one per camper
- Funnels
- Glue
- Optional: decorative pieces or stickers

What you do:
In a small bowl, pour the desired amount of salt. Using one color of sidewalk chalk, swirl it around in the salt, pressing down hard. Eventually, the salt will begin turning the color of the chalk. Once the salt is the desired color, place a funnel into the jar and pour the salt color inside. It should create a layer of color. Repeat the process again, using a different color. Once the jar has been completely filled, glue the lid to the jar by placing a line of glue on the outside edge of the jar and screw the lid on tight. The campers can then decorate their jars with stickers or decorative pieces.

Paper Maché Basket
Materials:

- Balloons
- Newspaper strips
- Liquid starch
- Paint tray
- Poster paints
- Large brushes
- Hole punch
- Yarn

What you do:
Pour the liquid starch into the paint tray. Blow a balloon up to the desired size and tie off. Dip a newspaper strip into the liquid starch and lay flat on the balloon. Repeat the process until the balloon is entirely covered. Let the balloon dry, leaving overnight. Once the paper maché is dry, pop the balloon inside. A hard bowl-like piece should be left. Punch a hole on each side, tying a piece of yarn across to make a basket or bucket. The camper can personalize his basket by painting it with the poster paints. Once the product dries completely, it can be used to gather items on a nature walk, collect a treasure during pirate night or hold prizes at the carnival.

Personalized Cups
Materials:

- Plastic cups
- Paint pens

What you do:
Lay out a variety of paint pens across the work table. Give each child a cup to personalize with his name, pictures or designs. Paint pens should dry within a few minutes and campers can take their cups with them back to the cabin.

Jewelry Creations
Materials:

- Clay or play-dough
- Toothpicks
- String

What you do:
Create small balls out of clay or play-dough. Push a toothpick into the center, making a small hole all the way through. Let the "jewels" dry overnight. Thread a string through the beads to create a necklace.

Note: This is a nice filler activity if campers finish another project early. Additionally, clay or play-dough can be available to make creations of any sort and left to dry over night.

Mural
Materials:

- Butcher paper
- Markers or crayons

What you do:
Place a sheet of butcher paper on the tables throughout camp to serve as a catch-all from projects. Throughout the week encourage campers to sign their name or draw a picture about camp as they finish other projects. At the end of the week, a campwide mural has been created. Display at closing ceremony if appropriate.

SENSORY ACTIVITIES

Shaving Cream Fun
Materials:

- Shaving cream, unscented
- Tarps
- Water hose

What you do:
Lay tarps out on the ground and spray with shaving cream. Campers can roll in the shaving cream or pick it up and throw it onto one another. Use additional cans of shaving cream to spray shaving cream directly into the campers' hands. A hair-do contest could be judged or the best design made on the tarp using the shaving cream. Be creative with contests. At the end, it is helpful to have a water hose nearby so that campers can be rinsed off before heading to the cabin or the next activity.

Water Fun
Materials:

- Balloons
- Buckets
- Water guns
- Sponges
- Sprinklers

What you do:
Create a water maze using sprinklers spraying in a variety of directions. Give campers sponges to dip in buckets of water and soak others. Water balloons and water guns could be available to add other ways of spreading the water. This activity should be carefully monitored for safety.

Slip-N-Slide
Materials:

- Tarp
- Sprinklers

What you do:
Lay several tarps secured to the ground with sprinklers towering over them. Line the campers up at one end and let them slide down the tarps to the other end.

Water Balloon Fun

Materials:

- Lots of water balloons
- Volleyball net
- Large spoons

What you do:

Create a variety of water balloon games.

Water balloon toss. Have the campers pair up, standing only a foot apart. Give each pair one water balloon. On the agreed-upon signal, each pair tosses the balloon to each other. Those whose balloon does not pop take one step back and repeat. Once a pair's balloon pops, they step to the side and cheer on their cabin mates.

Large spoon relay. Divide the campers into teams. Give each team one large spoon and a water balloon. One at a time, campers balance the water balloon on the large spoon, run down to a designated spot and run back. If the camper drops the balloon, a new one is placed on his spoon and he begins running again from where he dropped the first balloon.

Volleyball game. Divide the campers into two teams, one on each side of the net. Start with one water balloon. Have one team toss it to the other side as a serve, then proceed to throw it back and forth between team members up to three times before tossing it back over the net. If a water balloon pops or hits the ground, start a new serve with a fresh balloon.

Giant Parachute

Materials:

- Giant parachute
- Balls or water balloons

What you do:

Have each camper hold an edge of the parachute. (It can be lifted and pulled down a few times to demonstrate how it is used.) Number campers off, one through four. As the campers lift the parachute, a counselor calls a number, for example "three!" Campers who are number three let go and run underneath the parachute, changing places with another three, all before the parachute comes down. As an option to this game, instead of giving each camper a number, campers may be divided up by using a statement such as "this is my second year of camp." The campers who are included in the stated group let go of the parachute and change places with others belonging to the same group.

Balls or water balloons may also be used with the parachute. Campers holding the edge should begin to shake or slightly lift the parachute up and down. One at a time toss a ball onto the parachute, letting it bounce around. Encourage the campers to move the ball around, but not to let it fall off the parachute. Multiple balls or water balloons could be in motion at one time.

Relays
Materials:

- Bean bags
- Dry buckets
- Sponges
- Water bucket
- Medium-size ball

What you do:
Divide the campers into teams.

Bean bag relay. Spread the campers out with at least a foot of room between them. At one end of the line of campers, place a pile of bean bags. At the other end, place an empty bucket. On the agreed-upon signal, the first camper picks up a bean bag and tosses it to the next camper. The process continues down the line, concluding with the last camper tossing the bean bag into the bucket. The first camper begins tossing the second bean bag as soon as the hands of the camper behind him are empty. This relay is a rapid-motion game, but encourages focus, repetition, motor coordination and coordinated attention. If it becomes overwhelming, have the campers toss one bean bag all the way to the bucket before the next bean bag begins.

Sponge relay. Place the campers in a line. At the front of the line, place a bucket with water and one sponge. At the end of the line place an empty bucket with a line drawn inside. On the signal, the first camper dips the sponge into the bucket of water, soaking up as much water as possible. The sponge is then handed to each consecutive camper. When it reaches the last camper, he squeezes the remaining water into the finish bucket. Then he runs to the front of the line and dips the sponge into the bucket of water and begins again, handing the sponge to the camper behind him. This process continues until the water in the finish bucket reaches the designated line inside the bucket.

Ball hop relay. Line the campers up facing a finish line 10 feet away. The camper hops with a medium-size ball between his legs down to the finish line and back. Then he hands the ball off to the next camper. The sequence is repeated until all campers have made the hop.

Over-under relay. Bring the campers close together, still in a line. The first camper starts with a ball or water balloon and hands it over his head to the next camper. That camper passes the ball under his legs to the following camper, who hands it over his head to the following camper. The campers continue in the over-the-head, under-the-legs alternating pass until the camper at the end of the line receives the ball. He then runs to the front of the line and begins again. The relay is complete once all campers have run to the front.

Obstacle Course
Materials:

- Fabric tubes
- Bean bags
- Sidewalk chalk
- Foam squares
- Rubber jumpers
- Jump ropes

What you do:
Create an obstacle course using a variety of sensory objects. For example, use sidewalk chalk to create boundaries, a maze line to follow or hopscotch. Pile bean bags up or lay them out for the campers to jump over. Place the other items along the the course, encouraging campers to complete a task in order to move through the remainder of the course.

Giant Bubbles
Materials:

- Bubble solution
- Bubble blowers

What you do:
Lay out a variety of bubble blowers for the campers to use on their own. Additionally, large bubble blowers could be used to create numerous bubbles at one time. A large single bubble blower is always a hit among campers.

SOCIAL SKILLS/SELF-ESTEEM ACTIVITIES

Interviews
What to do:
As a group, discuss how to properly introduce oneself when meeting another person. Develop questions used to find out information about another person such as "what is your favorite movie?," "do you have any pets?," and so on, and write them on a large piece of paper or board for campers to refer to later. Pair campers off and ask them to interview their partners. Each camper should ask and answer five questions. Have a piece of paper and markers available so campers can create a visual if needed. A picture of the answer or the words may be drawn to help the campers remember the answers. When all pairs have completed the interview process, the whole group comes back together. Now each camper introduces his partner to the group, telling which questions were asked and the corresponding answer.

"I Am Special"
What you do:
Ask each camper to lie flat on a piece of butcher paper while a volunteer outlines his body. The camper can color in the picture to look like himself, adding clothes and a face. In addition, ask the camper to write things on the picture that make him special or his special gifts, such as writing "good listener" by his ears.

Compliments
What you do:
As a group, discuss what a compliment is, how it is used and why it is important. Place each child's name on a piece of paper in a bucket and ask each camper to pull out one name without telling anyone whose name he drew. The camper is then to come up with two to three compliments about the person whose name he drew and write them on the paper listing the name. Once everyone has finished, the group comes back together. One at a time the campers go around the circle reading the compliments, allowing the group to guess which camper is being described.

Oliver Onion

What you do:

Read the story *Oliver Onion: The Onion Who Learns to Accept and Be Himself* (Diane Murrell; Shawnee Mission, KS: Autism Asperger Publishing Company, 2004). Discuss as a group the meaning of the story and what happened. Ask the group if there has ever been anything they would like to change about their body or who they are. Discuss the importance of being just as they are. Allow the campers to illustrate the story, re-enact it or make a mural to gain the concept of the lesson.

Keeping Calm

What you do:

Brainstorm with the group things that make them calm or help them to relax. Write down the suggestions for campers to refer to. Also, ask the campers to list things that make them frustrated, angry or overwhelmed. Brainstorm and then role-play with them how to implement calming strategies in a variety of situations.

Solutions

What you do:

Using an incident or encounter that typically occurs at camp, real or fictional, play "what-if." As a group, have the campers brainstorm what else might happen, and what the possible solutions and outcomes to the situation would be. This allows the campers to realize that many factors affect a situation and that there are many solutions to each problem. After diagramming a few that are predetermined, ask the campers if they have any situations they would like to brainstorm about. Keeping calm strategies could be reiterated.

Today I Feel Silly

What you do:

To the group, read *Today I Feel Silly & Other Moods That Make My Day* (Jamie Lee Curtis; New York: Joanna Cotler Books, HarperCollins Publishers, 1998). As each page is read, have the campers identify the feeling being described and make a list. After the story is finished, discuss the feelings listed, defining any that are unfamiliar to the campers. Then, either as a group on a mural, or individually in a book, have the campers list the feeling and draw a picture or write words that express when they feel the named feeling. Discuss as a group when these feelings occur and how they make the campers feel on the inside, such as "that makes me feel fuzzy in my stomach," and what they do when they feel each one.

Role-Play or Skits

What you do:

Read an age-appropriate story or excerpt from a book, leaving the campers at a cliff hanger. Give them enough details to conceptualize the story, but allow them to create the ending themselves. Have the campers act out the story and come up with various endings and solutions. (Hanging signs with the characters' names around the campers' necks assists them in taking on a role.) Besides using a familiar story or characters, the counselors or campers can create action skits.

Appendix B
List of Games

Games
Backgammon
Candy Land
Catch Phrase
Checkers
Connect Four
Clue
Decks of cards
Dominoes
Go Fish
Guess Who
Guestures
Pictionary
Puzzles
Trouble
UNO

Movies
Babe
Blues Clues
Charlotte's Web
Elmo
Finding Nemo
Holes
Jungle Book
Lion King
Little Giants
Little Mermaid
Little Rascals: Mischief Loves Company
Lizzie McGuire
Mary Poppins
Monsters, Inc.
101 Dalmatians
Rookie of the Year
Tigger Movie
Toy Story
Willie Wonka and the Chocolate Factory

Books
Most campers will bring their own books; however, having a few varieties on hand is helpful. Choose an assortment of picture and chapter books that are currently popular among school-age and teenage children, both fiction and non-fiction.

Appendix C

Additional Resources

General Information

Attwood, T. (1998). *Asperger's Syndrome: A guide for parents and professionals*. London: Jessica Kingsley Publishers.

Janzen, J. (2003). *Understanding the nature of autism: A guide to the autism spectrum disorders. Second edition.* San Antonio, TX: Therapy Skill Builders.

Moore, S. T. (2002). *Asperger Syndrome and the elementary school experience: Practical solutions for academic and social difficulties.* Shawnee Mission, KS: Autism Asperger Publishing Company.

Myles, B. S., & Adreon, D. (2001). *Asperger Syndrome and adolescence: Practical solutions for school success.* Shawnee Mission, KS: Autism Asperger Publishing Company.

Behavior

Buron, K., & Curtis, M. (2004). *The incredible 5-point scale – Assisting students with autism spectrum disorders in understanding social interactions and controlling their emotional responses.* Shawnee Mission, KS: Autism Asperger Publishing Company.

Gagnon, E. (2001). *Power Cards: Using special interests to motivate children and youth with Asperger Syndrome and autism.* Shawnee Mission, KS: Autism Asperger Publishing Company.

Gray, C. (1994). *Comic strip conversations*. Arlington, TX: Future Horizons.

Gray, C. (1995). *Social stories unlimited: Social stories and comic strip conversations.* Jenison, MI: Jenison Public Schools.

Myles, B. S., & Southwick, J. (2005). *Asperger Syndrome and difficult moments: Practical solutions for tantrums, rage and meltdowns* (rev. expanded ed.). Shawnee Mission, KS: Autism Asperger Publishing Company.

Sensorimotor

Brack, J. (2004). *Learn to move, move to learn: Sensorimotor early childhood activity themes.* Shawnee Mission, KS: Autism Asperger Publishing Company.

Fuge, G., & Berry, R. (2004). *Pathways to play! Combining sensory integration and integrated play groups.* Shawnee Mission, KS: Autism Asperger Publishing Company.

Myles, B. S., Cook, K. T., Miller, N. E., Rinner, L., & Robbins, L. A. (2000). *Asperger Syndrome and sensory issues: Practical solutions for making sense of the world.* Shawnee Mission, KS: Autism Asperger Publishing Company.

Social

Baker, J. (2003). *Social skills training for children and adolescents with Asperger Syndrome and social-communication problems.* Shawnee Mission, KS: Autism Asperger Publishing Company.

Bieber, J. (Producer). (1994). *Learning disabilities and social skills with Richard LaVoie: Last one picked … first one picked on*. Washington, DC: Public Broadcasting Service.

Cardon, T. (2004). *Let's talk emotions: Helping children with social cognitive deficits, including AS, HFA, and NVLD, learn to understand and express empathy and emotions.* Shawnee Mission, KS: Autism Asperger Publishing Company.

Coucouvanis, J. (2005). *Super skills: A social skills group program for children with Asperger Syndrome, high-functioning autism and related challenges.* Shawnee Mission, KS: Autism Asperger Publishing Company.

Faherty, C. (2000). *What does it mean to me: A workbook explaining self-awareness and life lessons to the child or youth with high functioning autism or Asperger's.* Arlington, TX: Future Horizons.

Gagnon, E. (2001). *Power Cards: Using special interests to motivate children and youth with Asperger Syndrome and autism*. Shawnee Mission, KS: Autism Asperger Publishing Company.

Gray, C. (1994). *Comic strip conversations*. Arlington, TX: Future Horizons.

Gray, C. (1995). *Social stories unlimited: Social stories and comic strip conversations.* Jenison, MI: Jenison Public Schools.

Ives, M. (2001). *What is Asperger Syndrome, and how will it affect me? A guide for young people.* Shawnee Missions, KS: Autism Asperger Publishing Company.

Myles, B., Trautman, M., & Schelvan, R. (2004). *The hidden curriculum: Practical solutions for understanding unstated rules in social situations.* Shawnee Mission, KS: Autism Asperger Publishing Company.

Quill, K. A. (1995). *Teaching children with autism: Strategies to enhance communication and socialization.* London: International Thomas Publishing Company.

Wolfberg, P.J. (1999). *Play and imagination in children with autism.* New York: Teachers College Press.

Visuals

McClannahan, L., & Krantz, P. (1999). *Activity schedules for children with autism: Teaching independent behavior*. Bethesda, MD: Woodbine House.

Savner, J., & Myles, B. (2000). *Making visual supports work in the home and community: Strategies for individuals with autism and Asperger Syndrome.* Shawnee Mission, KS: Autism Asperger Publishing Company.

Peers/Siblings

Bleach, F. (2001). *Everybody is different – A book for young people who have brothers or sisters with autism*. Shawnee Mission, KS: Autism Asperger Publishing Company.